STORIES OF THE INDEBTED

STORIES

OF THE

INDEBTED

JORGE P. NEWBERY

Author of *Burn Zones* and *Debt Cleanse*

STORIES OF THE INDEBTED

Jorge P. Newbery

ISBN   978-1-61961-491-8   *Paperback*

978-1-61961-325-6   *Ebook*

Community
Books

Many of the stories you are about to read are based on true events, although characters may be composites. Some names and other information have been changed to protect the indebted.

CONTENTS

CHAPTER 1

HOW I SETTLED A $5,800,000 DEBT FOR $225,000

"HOW DID YOU SETTLE A $5,800,000 DEBT FOR $225,000?" A real estate broker named Shane cornered me after I finished speaking on a panel at a real estate crowdfunding conference. We were at One Financial Place under the stock exchange in downtown Chicago on September 18, 2014. For years, I hardly talked about my debt problems; now I was sharing my story with everyone who would listen.

On the panel, I spread the word about my company, American Homeowner Preservation, which purchases pools of nonperforming mortgages from banks at big discounts and then offers sustainable solutions to keep families in their homes. I also weaved in a few personal stories about my challenges with unaffordable debt. Those stories always proved to be the most popular portion of my talks. I was finding that success stories tend not to hold an audience's attention; listening to someone wax on about how great they are gets really dull really fast. Instead, people are riveted by failure—the greater the breakdown, the more intriguing the story.

Trudging ahead when everything is going wrong, not giving up when others would, and clawing back from collapse against extreme obstacles are what life's best stories are made of. At forty-nine, I was just learning that.

"A long, long time ago, when I was rich," I said, looking at Shane and a couple of others who had gathered around us at the refreshments table, "I bought a property called Woodland Meadows. This was 2002, and I obtained a $13.5 million mortgage from Vestin Mortgage. This was back when I paid my bills on time."

"I heard of Vestin," Shane said. Shane was short, pudgy, bespectacled, dark haired, and eager. He was probably in his late thirties and nicely dressed in a vested suit. Shane clutched a Styrofoam cup of coffee that was practically cream-colored as he spoke. "Their loans are costly."

"Yes, this was a one-year loan at twelve percent interest," I said. "But that was the only type of loan you could get on a property with poor occupancy, worse collections, and nicknamed Uzi Alley."

"That makes sense," chimed in a young Asian lady whose name tag read "Juju." She was in her late twenties and petite, with dark shoulder-length hair. She was sipping from a can of Diet Coke, which seemed odd, as she looked so lean already.

"I paid Vestin back exactly one year later on December 31, 2003, using the proceeds from a new mortgage funded with a municipal bond issue," I said. "Vestin then called me saying, 'It's very rare that our loans get paid off on time.' They told me they would be interested in financing my next project."

"Sounds like that deal worked out well for you and Vestin," said Shane.

"Yes," I said, between bites of pretzels. "So, in spring 2004, a bond broker offered me twenty million dollars' worth of bonds secured by a first mortgage on a large apartment complex in Austin, Texas, for ten million dollars. The project had not met income projections, and the payments had fallen behind, but it was still probably worth fifteen million dollars as is."

"That sounds like a good deal," said Juju. She started munching on a stick of celery without any dip.

"It was," I said. "I could buy the debt, try to get a deed-in-lieu from the owner, and soon own the property. I flew to Austin and walked this very large and well-situated complex. I was confident that I could utilize my hands-on management skills to turn the project around."

"Was this with American Homeowner Preservation?" asked Juju.

"No, this was well before AHP," I said. "I let the bond broker know that I would be proceeding. He said no one else was looking at the project yet. Then I called Vestin and asked them to finance my purchase. They were interested, and we agreed to terms similar to the Woodland Meadows loan. This was several months before the storm at Woodland Meadows, and I envisioned the Austin project as my next big challenge."

"You had it made," said Shane. "Made in the shade."

"Never think that. Never get comfortable," I said. "Vestin wanted to meet at the project and view it firsthand. I bought a cheap ticket on Southwest Airlines to fly from Columbus to Austin. Vestin's CEO, Michael Shustek, and one of their lead investors flew down in a private plane."

"Yowza," said Juju, sounding awed.

"Don't be impressed; that was all fluff," I said. "We toured the project, and they were visibly intrigued. We huddled at a nearby McDonalds. They stated that they were ready to fund the deal, but the terms were a bit different. The points, a loan fee based on a percentage of the loan amount, doubled, and the interest rate increased; plus they wanted a share of the profits."

"Bait and switch," said Shane.

"Exactly," I said. "I advised them that this was not what we had agreed to prior to flying down. They concurred, but said that they were only willing to proceed on the new terms."

"That used to happen with a lot of home-loan borrowers," said Shane.

"Yes, they get to the finish line of a long loan process only to be ambushed with new loan terms much worse than what they had been promised," I said. "Instead of giving in to Vestin's flagrant deception, I told them I would get the money elsewhere."

"Right move," said Juju.

"However," I said, "the following week the bond broker called me to tell me someone else bought the bonds."

"I thought no one else was looking at them," said Juju.

"That's what they had told me," I said. "I reasoned that there would be more opportunities."

"Too bad you lost out," said Juju. "That sounded like a good deal."

"It was," I said. "But the story took an unexpected turn."

"What happened?" asked Juju. Now she was downing a carrot, again without dip.

"Two months later, I called the Austin complex's apartment manager to see how the new owners were faring," I said. "She seemed surprised. She asked, 'Don't you know?' She then advised me that the new owners were the two guys I came to the property with—from Vestin.

"Is that illegal?" asked Shane.

"Get 'em," said Juju, impassioned. "You should have the cops arrestin' Vestin." We all laughed.

"I'm not sure about illegal, so no arrestin' Vestin," I

said. "Still, this was definitely unethical. I could have sued them and probably won. I called my attorney, who fired off a letter to Vestin threatening litigation."

"What happened?" asked Juju.

"We eventually agreed to a settlement in which Vestin paid me three hundred thousand dollars and agreed to provide me favorable financing terms on my next project," I said.

"Three hundred thousand dollars for going behind your back?" said Juju. "Not too bad."

"What next?" Shane asked.

"I bought Meridian Apartments, 248 units in Oklahoma City," I said. "Vestin made a $4.4 million loan secured by both a first mortgage on Meridian and a second mortgage on Pickwick, my 233-unit complex in Kansas City, which already had a five-million-dollar first mortgage administered by Wells Fargo."

"How good were the terms?" asked Shane before munching on a handful of M&M's.

"I forget the interest rate, but it was relatively low, and the points were either zero or close to it. This was probably the least-expensive loan that Vestin ever made," I said. "The term was for one year."

"How'd the project work out?" asked Juju, who was nibbling on a sprig of parsley. I was starting to really like Juju, particularly her dietary discipline.

"The renovation of Meridian went well," I said. "However, in late 2005, when the loan came due, I was nose deep in Woodland Meadows challenges and could not refinance." Woodland Meadows was hit by an ice storm on Christmas Eve 2004. The storm devastated the complex and, over time, the aftermath devastated me. "Vestin agreed to a six-month extension for a substantial fee, which I paid."

"Vestin should have extended the loan for free. They were backstabbers," said Juju. "You should have been contestin' Vestin." We all laughed.

"What happened next," Shane asked. He looked completely riveted.

"In May 2006, six months later, Woodland Meadows was almost empty, as were my pockets," I said. "Thus I could not refinance, and Vestin agreed to an additional 6-month extension."

"Did you have to pay again?" asked Juju.

"Yes," I said.

"Wǒ Kào," said Juju. We all looked at her. "Sorry, that's like 'dang' in Chinese."

"In November 2006, I was at my weakest point financially since I was a seven-year old paperboy," I said. "My extension ran out."

"Did they want another fee?" asked Juju.

"No, they wanted the property," I said. "Vestin advised that there would be no more extensions. They appointed a receiver to take over Meridian and collect the rents, and started foreclosure on both Meridian and Pickwick."

"*Wǒ Kào*," said Juju.

"*Wǒ Kào*," said Shane, mispronouncing the phrase slightly.

"Wow Kayo," I said, mauling the pronunciation. "Meridian is in Oklahoma, a judicial foreclosure state."

"The foreclosure has to go through the courts," said Shane. "Those go slow."

"That's right, so they filed a court case, and the foreclosure moved like a slug," I said. "On the other hand, Pickwick was in Missouri, a non-judicial foreclosure state," I said. "The Pickwick foreclosure moved rapidly. Pickwick was well occupied and financially performing well, and all the Wells Fargo first mortgage payments were up to date. The value was maybe six million dollars, but there was five million dollars due on the first mortgage."

"If Vestin foreclosed," said Shane, "they'd be responsible for the first mortgage payments."

"Exactly," I said. "Nevertheless, in January 2007, the Pickwick foreclosure sale was held. I sent a representative to the auction with the expectation that I could buy Vestin's position for a token amount."

"You'd be bestin' Vestin," said Juju, smiling. We laughed, but less this time, as her rhyme was not as funny. *You're wearing out your joke, Lil' Juju*, I thought.

"You were hoping to get it for a token," said Shane.

"Yes, I was connected with my representative by cell

phone and he bid ten thousand dollars to start the bidding," I said, focusing back on the story. "The very next bid came from Vestin's attorney: over $5.8 million, which was the full amount I owed plus all the egregious fees they had tacked on. I was disappointed that I had lost Pickwick."

"*Wǒ Kào*," we all said.

"That evening, I was running to relieve some stress when it hit me," I said. "I remembered that if a mortgage is secured by more than one piece of collateral, the lender must be careful to not bid their full indebtedness in order to avoid losing claims to the additional collateral."

"The $5.8 million was the full indebtedness," said Shane, catching on. "So if they used all their debt to buy Pickwick, there was no debt left on the Oklahoma City property."

"Exactly," I said. "I called my attorney the next day and asked him to call Vestin to congratulate them on their acquisition of Pickwick, but to ask that they release their mortgage on the Oklahoma property."

"So cool," said Juju, gleaming. "You won."

"Not yet," I said. "When Vestin realized their error, they filed a court action to set aside the sale they conducted."

"Assholes," said Juju. Shane and I looked at her; we were somewhat taken aback. "Sorry, but the people at Vestin really sound like jerks."

"Next, we filed a motion to dismiss Vestin's action, which the court granted," I said. "The court had ruled in our favor." Juju started applauding, and Shane joined in.

"No clapping yet," I said. "The fight was not over. Vestin then requested a meeting in Kansas City to try to work this out. Their attorney made a personal plea to me to the effect of, 'Doesn't taking advantage of Vestin's error seem unfair?' I shared the Austin story with him and then asked if Vestin's backstabbing seemed fair."

"You were molestin' Vestin," said Juju, who started laughing though no one else did. The joke had hit the wall.

"I then shared my observation that people get treated the way they treat others," I said. "And, given that, taking advantage of Vestin's error actually felt very fair."

"Was that the end?" asked Shane.

"No," I said. "Vestin appealed to the state court of appeals."

"I'm surprised they didn't give up already," said Juju.

"In a unanimous ruling," I said, "the appeals court judges sided with me."

"You won!" said Juju, raising her arms wide open like she wanted to hug me. I gave her a light hug and, with my arm around her, I marveled at how thin she really was. Then I shook Shane's hand.

"In order to avoid further court action," I said. "Vestin agreed to settle their debt of over $5,800,000 for $225,000."

"That's a good story," Shane said. "But I cannot imagine that kind of mistake comes up often."

I nodded. "That was a unique set of circumstances," I

said. "But every debt has a unique set of circumstances, and creditors are constantly making errors. You just need to find the errors and exploit them."

"I need to take out more loans," said Juju. "Then find the errors and settle them at discounts."

"The better idea is to not take on any more debt," I said. "Exploit the deficiencies to get out of debt you may already have and cannot afford."

"Makes sense," said Juju, who then emptied her Diet Coke.

"The Vestin resolution was my first really big victory against a creditor," I said. "It was a turning point for me and gave me the resolve to take on other creditors."

"Did you win more?" Shane asked.

"Yes, I had many other wins," I said. "All of which continued to build my confidence. Now I believe I can take on any debt, find issues, and settle."

"Do you still have debts to fight?" asked Juju.

"I have a couple of big debt fights going on," I said. "However, I am running out of my own debts to fight. Now I help others settle their unaffordable debts."

"You're the threat to debt," said Juju. "The Debt Threat."

We all laughed.

Another attendee came up. His name tag read "Jeffrey."

"I enjoyed hearing you on the panel," he said. "I have just one question: How did you settle a $5,800,000 debt for $225,000?"

Shane, Juju, and I all smiled.

CHAPTER 2

MORTGAGES AT STARBUCKS

"HI, MR. NEWBERY," A FEMALE VOICE SAID.

Emily was one of my good friends. Back in 2012, she had phoned me and asked to meet to discuss the difficulty she was having with her mortgage. A divorced mom of three, Emily was struggling to make ends meet. Still, she looked well as she approached me at a nearby Starbucks. She was a buxom brunette with a ready smile. I knew she was around fifty years old, but if she had told me she was forty, I would have believed her.

"Oh," I said, "Hi, Emily." I stood up to give her a quick hug. "How are you doing?"

"I need help with my mortgage," she said, sounding anxious. Emily lived in a nice home in Glendale, California, with her three children.

"Are you still in your home?" I asked

"Yes," she said. "For now at least."

She told me her lender had already advised that they would accept a short sale of $450,000, which was the market value of her home. She owed $600,000 and wanted me to find an investor to purchase her home on a short sale and lease it back to her with an option to repurchase.

"Is that even possible?" she said.

"There's a much better way, actually," I said.

Emily's eyes got wide. "Better? How so? My lender said selling the home was the only option if I can't pay. What is your plan?"

"Well, the first step is to stop paying," I said. "I guess you got that covered."

"Yes, that was the easy part," said Emily, letting out a nervous laugh.

"Next, ask your mortgage company for a modification," I said. "This usually delays the start of foreclosure."

Many mortgage companies will not seriously consider modifications until you are at least thirty or sixty days delinquent. If you are current on your mortgage, lenders typically assume that you can either afford your mortgage or you value your credit score so much that you will not let an unpaid mortgage blemish your credit report.

"I can do that," she said.

"The good news is that majority of lenders and servicers are unbelievably slow in processing modification requests, so relish the delays," I said. "Delays are your new best friend."

"So I want them to go slow?" she said, leaning forward to hear more clearly as a large truck rumbled by.

"Yes, you will gain value every day you stay in your home without paying," I said. "You can put more and more payments in your settlement wallet."

"Two problems there," said Emily. "First, I can't afford the payment."

"What can you comfortably afford each month?" I said.

"Maybe a thousand dollars?" she said.

"A thousand dollars it is then," I said.

"Okay. Second, what's a settlement wallet?" she said.

"Well, for one thing, it's not a physical wallet. Though I suppose it could be," I said and then took a sip of my green smoothie. "I'm thinking more in terms of a PayPal account, a separate bank account, an attorney, or even a friend or family member."

She nodded. I could tell she was already thinking of where she would set aside her $1,000. I continued: "You just need to set aside the money so that you do not spend it on other stuff. That way, you have the money to settle or modify the loan, or pay legal fees, when you need it. The longer you go without paying, the fatter your settlement wallet gets."

"I like this idea," she said.

"So now you realize that time is on your side and delays are in your best interest?" I said, relaxing back in my chair a bit. I looked around, and my eyes caught a group of runners running down the street at a good clip. *I would like to be on a run right now,* I thought to myself.

"I will welcome delays," she said.

"You can help make your mortgage company process your modification even slower," I said.

"How?" she said.

"Always reply to everything they request near the end of the deadline," I said. "For example, they'll probably ask you to provide two updated paystubs within thirty days. Even if you have them handy and could submit that day, hold on to them. Instead, wait until day twenty-five."

"I'd pick up twenty-five days?" she said.

"Exactly," I said. "This may not seem like much, but if you answer every request at the end of the deadline, you can probably pick up a few months."

"Awesome," said Emily.

"You can even send in out-of-date paystubs at the end of the deadline," I said. "Then they'll probably send you a new request for current paystubs, giving you another thirty days."

"This is funny," she said, giggling. "Kind of like playing footsies. There is excitement, like something is going to happen, but nothing actually does. If you just keep wiggling your toes, the mortgage company thinks something is happening."

"But all you're doing is wiggling," I said. "You're not actually moving forward."

"I can wiggle," she said.

"I'm sure you can," I said. "Most mortgage companies are really inefficient when it comes to processing modifications. They will often go back and forth dozens of times in this mind-numbing game of, well, footsies. This paper circus can go on for months or years, with the mortgage company apparently oblivious to the fact that their delays are costing them or their investors millions of dollars."

"What if they approve my modification after all my wiggling?" she said after draining the last of her espresso.

"They might, but the mod will most likely be of little benefit to you," I said. "Most mod requests are denied. When approved, they often do not include principal reductions, the payment is modestly lower if not higher, the loan is longer, and the back payments are frequently tacked onto the end of the loan. No benefit."

"What if they give me an Obama mod?" she said.

"You mean the federal government's Home Affordable Mortgage Program?" I asked. "This is more commonly known as HAMP because the program hampers homeowners who want to stay in their homes."

"Really?" Emily asked. "It hampers?"

"Yes," I said and then took a sip from my smoothie. "HAMP provides taxpayer subsidies to lenders to modify loans on terms that are barely affordable for homeowners and rarely provide principal reductions. HAMP is a lender handout disguised as a homeowner assistance program. There's little benefit to homeowners, even though many accept the bad deal out of desperation to stay in their homes."

"Okay, so I don't want that," she said. "So what should I tell them?"

"Tell them you want a modification with the principal reduced to $427,500—five percent less than the current value," I said. "And a payment that is very affordable. You said you can put one thousand dollars monthly into your settlement wallet, so say you want the payment to be one thousand dollars."

"I doubt they would accept that," she said.

"Probably not, but that's why you say no to their offer, and then we work to create some leverage," I said. "Your goal is that they will eventually agree to your offer. In the interim, whether you are denied for a mod or if you are approved and refuse to accept their terms, they will likely terminate your mod request."

"What will I do next?" she said.

"Stop talking to them," I said.

"Really?" she said. "They seem to be trying to help."

"They are trying to get you to pay a mod with a balance higher than your home value and a payment you cannot afford," I said. "That's not helping."

"They call a lot," she said. "What do I say to them?"

"Nothing," I said. "Just hang up."

"You're kidding, right?" she said, incredulous.

"No, seriously, just hang up," I said. "Then download a call blocking app like Call Control on your phone so then they won't be able to get through anymore."

"Won't that just make the mortgage company mad?" she said.

"Most of the mortgage companies are too big to get mad," I said. "The collector or automated system making the call just moves on to the next delinquent borrower. Who really cares if they get mad? I'm mad at the banks, and I don't think they care."

"I'm mad at them too," said Emily. "But what about all the letters?"

"I hate the banks as well," said a red-haired lady in her forties seated next to us in jeans and a black top. She was lean and fit and looked like she might be a runner. "Sorry, I wasn't eavesdropping. I just overheard a bit about trying to get a mortgage modification. I tried that with Chase, and they turned me down, foreclosed on me. Totally fucked up my life. I got divorced right after that. Fuck the banks."

"Sorry to hear that," I said. Emily and I looked at each other, a bit startled.

"I hope everything gets better for you," Emily said.

"Thanks, I'm getting by," the redhead said. "Sorry, again, I didn't mean to interrupt."

Emily and I snuck a glance at one another. Though the woman's interruption was unexpected, her story was certainly not unfamiliar. It seems just about everyone knows someone who went through a similar experience.

"So what do I do with the letters?" asked Emily again.

"Just keep them in a file," I said.

"So I pretend I'm dead, more or less?" she said skeptically.

"Or that you are on an extended vacation," I said.

"I could sure use a vacation now," she said. "Even not taking their calls will be like a holiday. These guys are stressing me out. They pass me from department to department and no one appears to have any authority."

"Don't stress," I said. Just then I heard an audible chirp. It must have been Emily's cell notifying her of a new text.

"Hold on," she said as she typed on her smartphone. A couple of cyclists rolled up to Starbucks wearing Velo Club La Grange jerseys. That was my first cycling club back in 1985. I thought to say something, but they both looked to be in their early twenties. They probably weren't even born when I was a member. I felt old.

"Sorry, that was my daughter," she said. "We are making plans for my eldest son's birthday party."

"No problem," I said. "How old will he be?"

"Twenty-one," she said. "I feel old."

"You and me both," I said.

"Well, so far you have told me pretty much to buy time," she said. "When do I get to actually *do* something?"

"Doing something is the next step. Your lender will send you a demand letter, probably giving you thirty days to pay," I said. "This is required in all states."

"I think I got that already," she said. "It said something like notice of acceleration."

"That's it," I said. "Demand letters and notices of acceleration are typically the same. When did you get it?"

"A couple of weeks ago," she said. "What is it?"

"It's the first step in the foreclosure process," I said. "I need you to send your lender a qualified written request."

"What's that?" asked Emily.

"Fifteen pages with dozens of questions for your servicer," I said. "Just fill in a few blanks at the top with your loan info and then sign at the bottom and mail it in. Here, let me pull a sample up on my phone and I can show you."

"Looks tedious," Emily said, as she scrolled through the QWR on my phone. "What are 'suspense, unapplied transactions?'"

"That's when you make a payment, but your servicer does not apply the funds," I said. "The money sits in suspense. For instance, if you make a half payment, your lender would likely put this in suspense until the other half is received at some later date. Still, don't worry if you don't recognize some of the terms. That's for the mortgage company to figure out."

"Do they have to answer all this?" she said.

"Yes, they have to answer everything that is applicable," I said. "Basically, you are asking them to prove that you owe what they allege."

"Well, I do owe the money," she said, sounding a bit resigned and slumping back in her chair.

"That's not the point," I said. "Your creditor needs to prove exactly what you owe, who actually owns the loan, and provide evidence that they have the documents and records to prove it."

"Well, the loan was with Countrywide but is now with Bank of America," she said. "Those are two huge companies, so I expect that their records are straight." I started laughing out loud.

"What's funny?" she asked.

"I'll bet we will find problems," I said. "The big banks are the worst."

"Well, I've heard the stories about Goldman Sachs and some of the banks that got in trouble, but I have banked with Bank of America for years," she said. "I trust them. Or, at least, I don't think they are as bad."

"If 'trust' means that you don't question them, then that's about to end. All the big banks have betrayed us," I said. "Just fill out the QWR and send in, and then we'll see how good their records and documents are. Send one via certified mail, and keep a copy."

"Consider it done," she said, perking up. "So essentially I just answer their demand with a demand of my own. Sounds reasonable. What next?"

"Just wait for their response and let me know if they start foreclosure," I said.

"Can they start foreclosure before they answer my demand?" she said. "I mean qualified whatever?" She was looking a little nervous again.

"Yes, they can still start foreclosure," I said. "But they might think twice if you have submitted the qualified written request and they cannot answer everything. They may not have the ability to foreclose if all their documents and records are not in order."

"Have you ever completed one?" she asked.

"Yes, we've received a few at AHP," I said. "Total hassle. Many times, documents get lost and figures get fuzzy as documents and data are transferred among different mortgage companies. Fully answering a QWR can be challenging and time-consuming."

"So how long before I hear back?" she said.

"The mortgage company is required to respond or at least acknowledge receipt of the request within five business days," I said. "And, within thirty business days, they are required to provide the information you requested, let you know why they cannot provide it, or extend the response period by fifteen days."

"What if they don't respond?" she said.

"Then you can sue them for your damages," I said.

"What are my damages?" she asked.

"Well, right now you are living for free, so no real damage yet," I said. "But if they try to foreclose and they didn't properly respond, this may give you leverage."

"I need leverage," she said.

"Exactly," I said. "You need as much leverage as you can get so that we can try to get Bank of America to either give you a great mod with affordable payments and reduced principal, or sell your loan to someone who will."

"You know, I have some friends who are also having trouble with their Bank of America mortgages," she said. "I wonder if they could do the same thing?"

"The same tactics apply no matter which bank you have," I said. "The debts could be with Bank of America or any creditor."

"What if all of the Bank of America borrowers who cannot afford their mortgages all send in QWRs on the same day," she said. "They couldn't keep up, could they?"

"Depends on how many, but this could be paralyzing for lenders," I said, laughing at her anarchist streak. "We should get all mortgage borrowers with all lenders to send in QWRs on the same day. Responding to all the requests at once would be a big challenge for the banks."

"They deserve it. They're the ones giving everyone else big challenges," Emily said. "We should do it."

I smiled at her. "We'll start spreading the good word and see if it catches on."

Emily started laughing again and then quickly settled back into her focus mode. "So what's Bank of America going to do after denying my deliberately failed, but time-rewarding, mod application and the silent treatment I will give them?"

"Okay," I said. "At some point, Bank of America starts foreclosure."

"In the meantime, I have stayed in my house for free for months, or even years, and my settlement wallet is overflowing," she said.

"Yes. So now you prepare for foreclosure," I said.

"How do I prepare for that?" she said with a touch of nervousness creeping back into her voice.

"Expect it. It's really just important to know that foreclosure is coming."

"Okay, consider me prepared," she said. "What's next?"

"Well, you are in California, so you will get a notice of default," I said. "This is recorded with the county recorder, and you'll get copies by certified mail." California is a non-judicial state, meaning that foreclosures can be handled outside of the court system. Other states, such as Illinois where I live, are judicial states, which require lenders to file foreclosure lawsuits in court. Borrowers in judicial states will receive a lawsuit and have a prescribed period, often twenty-eight days, to respond. Judicial foreclosure is generally better for borrowers.

"What do I do then?" she said.

"Find an attorney to file a lawsuit against Bank of America," I said. "And request a temporary restraining order to stop any foreclosure sale."

"And I use the money in my settlement wallet to pay the attorney?" she said.

"Exactly," I said. "You're a fast learner."

"Well, you're a good teacher," she said.

"Aww, thanks," I said playfully.

"So how do I find an attorney—a good one?" she said.

"We are going to start a listing of attorneys on my site, debtcleanse.com, and include reviews, as well as provide attorneys training in Debt Cleanse strategies," I said. "In the meantime, search online and look for a law firm with success representing other families in foreclosure. Maybe check for reviews on Yelp."

"And my attorney will make all my problems go away?" she said.

"No, attorneys are like tools," I said. "They can help, and in some cases are essential, but you are your own magic bullet."

"I'm a bullet?" she said.

"What I mean is, your attorney may be working for you, but you need to stay in contact, be responsive to the law firm's requests, and make sure they are working your case as effectively as possible," I said. "Ultimately, your success is dependent on you."

"Kind of a team, like a good marriage?" she asked. "Both sides need to contribute in order to succeed."

"Yes," I said. "Kind of like a good marriage. To start, upload to debtcleanse.com whatever documents you have from when you first took out the loan," I said. "Plus all the correspondence you've received, your monthly statements, a log of your calls, and whatever they send you back in response to the QWR."

"Okay," she said. "I haven't been keeping a call log, and some of the letters I put in the trash."

"Do the best you can," I said. "Input what you remember from any calls and just upload what you have."

"Got it," she said. "What's going to happen with all of those documents?"

"You can share access to them with your attorney, if you need to file suit," I said. "Then you and your attorney can look for deficiencies, find any errors, and determine what documents the lender appears to lack," I said. "Anything that can create leverage against your lender."

"Okay," she said. As I pondered what Emily was about to face, I remembered a recent article I'd read.

"Hey, I'm going to e-mail you a link to an article," I said. "This might give you some inspiration."

"You are my inspiration, Mr. Newbery," she said. I think I detected sarcasm in her voice somewhere.

"Well, thanks," I said. "I just e-mailed it to you. A jury awarded $16.2 million to a California homeowner because they made an error caused by six hundred and sixteen dollars."

"Was that six hundred and sixteen thousand dollars?" she asked, picking up her phone.

"No, six hundred and sixteen dollars," I said. "Then they refused to fix the error."

"I'm opening it now," Emily said, her interest audibly piqued.

The article revealed that flaws in a servicer's record-keeping and processing were recently exposed in a July 2014 jury award of $16.2 million in damages to a California homeowner because of the servicer's refusal to correct an error caused by $616. In 2011, Phillip Linza, a salesman from Plumas Lakes, California, received a loan modification from servicer PHH Corp. However, a $616 shortfall in Linza's escrow account, used to pay property taxes and insurance as part of the monthly payment, caused PHH's computer systems to generate letters automatically that demanded different amounts each month.

When Linza called PHH to inquire about the inconsistent payment requests and to ask for a simple letter verifying the correct amount due, PHH refused to assist. Eventually, even though the modification reduced his monthly payment to $1,543, PHH sent him a letter demanding $7,056. Linza eventually threatened to sue PHH. Their response "was to tell him to go ahead, file a lawsuit, and get in line because they had deeper pockets than he had to litigate this," according to Linza's attorney, Andre Cherney.

"PHH wouldn't own up to their own mistake and find a reasonable solution, which was to do the decent act of writing a letter to clarify everything," said Jon Oldenburg, who also represented Linza. "It's a pretty consistent theme that servicers in this context very rarely admit that they've done anything wrong," Oldenburg added. "You don't see many servicers own up to their part in the process. They think that because the borrower went into default, they don't have any legal claims."

"This guy Linza's experience is common," I said. "Errors and borrower abuse by big banks and servicers are rampant. Thus the environment is ripe for you to challenge them."

"Sounds like it," Emily said. "Can you teach me how to get $16.2 million?"

"I'm not sure about that. PHH is appealing Linza's award, so it will probably end up less anyway," I said. "However, I can teach you how to stay in your home and maximize the odds that you receive a viable solution from your mortgage company. A good start to this is the QWR as well as documenting all your calls and correspondence with your servicer. Create a file for the correspondence and a ledger identifying the day and time of calls and voice-mails, as well as what was said."

"Maybe I should record them?" Emily said.

"Yes, you can get a mobile phone app to do that," I said.

"So when the creditor says, 'This call may be recorded'," she said, enthusiastically. "Then I can say, 'This call may be recorded back, suckers?'"

"Well, maybe leave the 'suckers' part out," I said. "But otherwise, yes."

"You still didn't tell me how to get $16.2 million," Emily said.

"All I can do is show you how to create leverage," I said. "And you can use the leverage to get an affordable modification with permanent interest, payment, and principal reductions; time in the home living for free; or even a cash award in court. This depends on how much leverage you can build."

"And I hold out until I get the deal that definitely makes sense for me," she said. "How long will this take?"

"It could take years," I said.

"And all the while I get to stay in my home with my kids," she said, smiling with relief. Her face was glowing. "Thanks, Mr. Newbery."

Emily owed over $600,000 on a home worth $450,000. She was "underwater" and had negative equity. One in five American homeowners with a mortgage are in this predicament. That's over ten million families who, if they sold their homes, would not generate enough sales proceeds to pay off their mortgage debts. The negative equity plague is particularly acute in many predominantly minority low- and moderate-income communities. For instance, more than fifty percent of the homes in Ferguson, Missouri are underwater. Yet for the last few years, the headlines have portrayed a different picture, one of recovery and reclamation, as though the housing crisis were a thing of the past. And if we choose to look only at the neighborhoods they've chosen to spotlight, it's easy to believe them. If we choose to live in the real world, however, the picture is very different. This is why I started American Homeowner Preservation.

Few things are as satisfying to me as being able to help others work themselves out from under their unaffordable debt, but being able to help a close friend like Emily made my job even better. As we parted ways, I reminded her to keep me updated.

"And, of course, if there are any issues, don't hesitate to call me."

"Let's hope it never comes to that," she said and smiled.

* * *

"MR. NEWBERY, I NEED YOUR HELP."

It was September 2014, and I had received a call from Emily asking if we could meet again. Her timing was perfect, as I was already in California for a speaking opportunity. Now we were at the Cheesecake Factory on San Vicente. I looked outside and witnessed the gray, drizzling weather.

"Wow, it's raining. I didn't know you had rain in California."

"Yes," said Emily. "We bring rain back once in a while, for old time's sake."

"A little meteorological nostalgia," I said. "So how can I help?"

"Well, I did everything you suggested," she said. Emily looked older. "It's been two years since I last made a payment. The kids and I are still in our home."

"I'm glad to hear that," I said.

"Me too," she said. "It has worked out like you forecasted. Bank of America approved me for a modification, but it was completely whack. My payment actually went *up*, they added years to my loan, and my principal balance increased. Not helpful at all."

"Whack modification?" I asked. "I like that. I might use it."

"When my mortgage is settled, you can have it," she said. "I'm exhausted. I'm tired of playing financial footsies. I want to know when this is going to end."

"You need to be patient," I said.

"I have been paying the attorney a thousand dollars a month, which is much less than rent or what the whack modification would be," she said. "We even found some deficiencies to exploit. I've done everything you suggested."

"Great," I said.

"But the uncertainty is eating away at me," Emily said.

"I know," I said. "I used to grind my teeth when Woodland Meadows was collapsing. That's why you're getting tired of wiggling. Me, I've been wiggling for years. You've gone less than two years, which is barely a 5K. Think of your Debt Cleanse like a marathon."

"But what can I do to get to the finish line faster?" she asked.

"Nothing," I said. "You have an attorney. You filed a lawsuit. You delayed the foreclosure sale. You're exploiting deficiencies. You're doing everything right. Just be patient."

"You make it sound easy," she said.

"It's not easy, but you need to endure," I said. "What is the negative impact of your unresolved mortgage situation on your daily life?"

There was silence.

"Okay, well maybe it's not bad right now," she said. "But sometimes I worry about what is going to happen."

"You can only do what is best for you in the moment," I said. "Don't worry what might happen in the future, because you cannot control that. Deal with the problem in front of you. That's what you can deal with."

"Okay, Dr. Newbery," she said.

"I'm not a doctor," I said. "But I can tell you that the longer you stay, the longer you go without paying, the better the likelihood that you will have a positive outcome."

"But what kind of guarantee can I get that this will have a happy ending?" she asked.

"None. No guarantees," I said. "But no matter what happens, you are better off than if you took the whack modification you were offered early on."

"True. I couldn't have kept up with those payments," she said. "I would have been in trouble right away."

"If you did a short sale, you'd have gotten nothing," I said. "Same if you moved voluntarily, or let it go to foreclosure."

"I guess so," said Emily.

"You haven't paid your mortgage in two years," I said. "Instead, you are paying a thousand a month to an attorney to fight the bank. To rent a similar home would cost double or even more."

"That's right," she said.

"You are way ahead. You already won," I said. "You gained all this time and put some cash in your settlement wallet. How much are you up to?"

The waitress arrived with our lunch.

"Well, most has been going to the attorney," she said before she took a bite of her dish. "I had a few thousand from before I hired the attorney, but something happened to it."

"*Something* happened to it?" I asked then took my first mouthful of angel hair pasta. "What happened to it?"

"Well..." she said, hesitating

"Emily, what happened to the cash in your settlement wallet?" I said, putting down my fork and pressing the matter.

"Well, Connie graduated from high school last June," she said, sounding ashamed. "And it seemed like a great time for a family vacation. I used the money in the settlement wallet."

"Emily, you were supposed to keep the settlement wallet out of your clutches," I said. "I thought you were going to give it to a friend or put in a separate PayPal account."

"I did. I put it in a separate PayPal account just like you said. And it just sat there and sat there," she said. "And sat there."

"Until you took it out for the family vacation?" I said.

"Yes," she said, sounding like a kid who just got caught sneaking an extra helping of cheesecake. "We had a really good time."

"Well," I said, hesitatingly. "That was probably a once-in-a-lifetime opportunity."

"Yes, better to use the money to take my family on holiday than to pay Bank of America," she said.

"Yes, Americans need to stop slaving away to pay creditors," I said. "Spend some time with the family, take some trips. Do you feel better? Are you ready to keep going in this marathon?"

"Yes, I'm in it to win it," she said. "I'll see you at the finish line."

"That's the attitude," I said. "I'm rooting for you."

Just then a woman approached our table. Emily smiled and stood up to hug her.

"Alexis!" Emily turned back to me, "This is Alexis, my best friend."

I looked up and saw Alexis. She looked Puerto Rican, late thirties, about five feet ten, and attractively curvy.

She was wearing tight jeans and, as she took off her jacket, she revealed a snug-fitting tank top. I noticed a table of three guys next to us checking her out.

Emily motioned to her to sit down. I had the funny feeling that I was being set up and hoped it was not for a reason that would require a lot of explanation to my wife, Verria. I wiped my hands on my napkin, stood up, and shook Alexis' hand.

"Hi, Alexis," I said.

"Hi, Mr. Newbery," said Alexis in a thick Puerto Rican accent.

"You can call me Jorge," I said.

"I kind of like Mr. Newbery," Alexis said, laughing. "Sounds distinguished."

"Alexis is visiting from Cleveland, Ohio, and has a problem like mine," Emily said.

"Yes, I lost my job last year and haven't found a new one yet. I fell behind on my mortgage," Alexis said, recounting a familiar story across America.

"Our government keeps saying unemployment is getting lower, but I don't see it," I said.

"For real," Alexis said. "I was a legal secretary for eighteen years at the same firm, making good money. Now I am vying for jobs alongside recent college grads who are still living at home with their parents. Their expenses are so much lower than they get later in life, with kids and all,"

"I lived at home with my parents for my first several

years in real estate," I said. "I saved a lot of money."

"Yes, they can work for lower salaries, even free internships," Alexis said. "It's hard to compete. Plus, potential employers keep saying I am overqualified. I have started dumbing down my resume. I think that might help."

"Sad. All your qualifications don't help if no one is hiring," I said. "What can I do to help?"

"Well, my loan is with Ocwen," Alexis said.

"Sorry to hear that," I said. "They may be the worst servicer in the country."

"Actually, I think they are in India," Alexis said.

"Well, they are based in the US, but you are partially right," I said. "The majority of their operations are in India and Venezuela."

"They are horrible to work with," said Alexis.

"Ocwen was just accused of backdating thousands of letters denying modifications to homeowners," I said. "By backdating, Ocwen was able to proceed with foreclosures without waiting for borrowers' appeal periods to pass."

"That's awful," said Emily.

"Terrible," said Alexis.

"Well, maybe some homeowners can use Ocwen's fraud to gain some leverage," I said. "So there might be a silver lining to this."

"Welcome to the Cheesecake Factory," our waitress said to Alexis as she arrived at our table. "What can I get you?"

"Veggie burger with cheese, no bun," said Alexis. "And corn succotash as the side."

"Got it." The waitress wrote down the order, turned, and sauntered away.

"I hope you don't mind me just showing up like this," Alexis said to me. "I told Emily I wanted to meet you after she told me how you have been coaching her on how to not pay and still stay in her home."

"It would mean a lot to both of us if you could help, Mr. Newbery," Emily said.

"Okay," I said. "Alexis, I will share the basics. If you have questions, call Emily first, as she may have already been through the step. But if you run into something Emily does not know, then call me." I recalled that this is how Alcoholics Anonymous works. Debt Cleanse could work the same way: as debtors make progress, they can share their experiences with others in similar situations.

"Okay," said Alexis, sounding giddy.

"You already stopped paying," I said.

"Check," said Alexis.

"I presume that Ocwen has been calling you a lot," I said.

"Oh God yes," Alexis said. "I think I need to change my number."

"Have you been served with the foreclosure lawsuit?" I asked. "Ohio is a judicial state."

"Not yet," said Alexis.

"A judicial state?" asked Emily.

"Yes, Ocwen will need to file a lawsuit in court in order to foreclose on Alexis," I said. Judicial foreclosures tend to be more costly and time-consuming for lenders and, as a result, generally provide more protections to borrowers.

"But I had to file the lawsuit to stop the foreclosure on my home," Emily said.

"Yes, that's because California is non-judicial," I said. "California foreclosures can be handled outside of the courts. But if you as the borrower sue the lender, then you effectively put the foreclosure into the courts."

"So, using your tactics, all the foreclosures end up in court, even if they are in non-judicial states?" Emily asked.

"Exactly," I said.

"Excellent," said Emily.

"Alexis?" I asked.

"Yes, Coach?" Alexis said, enthusiastically.

"Have you received a demand letter yet?" I asked.

"I'll have to look through all the mail," she said.

"Well, if you haven't paid in a year, then you should go ahead and send in a QWR," I said.

"Why doesn't she wait for QWR Day?" asked Emily, sounding serious.

"Good idea," I said. "Alexis, if you have not received a demand letter and you don't get one soon, then go ahead and send in on QWR Day."

"QWR Day?" Alexis asked, evidently befuddled.

"What's QWR Day?"

"That's the day when everyone in America with an unaffordable mortgage will mail in a QWR to their mortgage companies," said Emily, delighted with her plan. "We are going to paralyze banks and mortgage companies."

"What does QWR stand for?" asked Alexis.

"Qualified Written Request," Emily said. "Kind of like truth or dare: the mortgage companies need to tell the truth on like one hundred questions. You're telling them, 'I dare you to foreclose. I'm about to make your life miserable.'"

"Well, more or less," I said. "The QWR is helpful in identifying deficiencies and errors made by the lender. The overall strategy is to identify deficiencies in the loan documents, legal pleadings, and records of the lender and then exploit these to slow down or stop the foreclosure."

"Sounds fun," Alexis said. "You know, with my legal background, I can help others find deficiencies if you show me what to look for." I started pondering the overall Debt Cleanse strategy I was formulating: we can share our journey with other participants. Each of us can contribute our own knowledge, skills, and talents for the greater good.

"Sounds like how a society should work," I said.

"Tell me, what sort of deficiencies should I be looking for?" Alexis asked, looking at me.

"Here's what my attorney and I found," said Emily. "The assignment of my loan was signed by a robo-signer.

We found that out by Googling the names of everyone who signed documents in my file and by adding robosigner to the end. Also, the signer works in Georgia, but the document was notarized in Minnesota. It's possible that the signer flew to Minnesota to sign my document, but we doubt it. My attorney is trying to depose the signer and notary."

"That all sounds typical," I said.

"Also, the signature was just two big circles," Emily said. "It looks like a little kid was playing with a crayon. It does not look like a real signature. Plus, the signer wrote February 21, 2011, next to her name, but the notary part stated that she signed on April 6, 2011."

"Really, that sounds like fraud," Alexis said. "I'm a notary, and you can't notarize a signature six weeks late."

"That's what we thought," Emily said. "So we contacted the secretary of state in Minnesota and requested a copy of the notary's application. Guess what?"

"What?" Alexis asked.

"The signatures on her notary application and on my assignment were totally different," Emily said.

"No!" Alexis said sounding stunned.

"Yep," Emily said. "The signatures were totally different, like looking at Whitney Houston before she met Bobby Brown and then after they were together all those years."

"May Whitney rest in peace," said Alexis. "Bobby was no good for her."

"Yes, he's a scoundrel," said Emily. "She deserved better."

"Wow, you have a fake notary on a robo-signed document," said Alexis. "Tell your bank they should give you the house for free. Just release the mortgage."

"Free houses probably will not happen," I interjected. "But Emily is creating major leverage. She should be able to parlay that into a good solution."

"There's more," said Emily, teasingly after she took a sip of water.

"What other dirt did you dig up?" asked Alexis.

"So Bank of America filed a notice of default with the county," said Emily. "The document has the same loops, like a kid drew it. My attorney says that whoever signs the notice of default is supposed to review the document and verify that all the information in the document is accurate," said Emily, earnestly. "Plus, the notice of default was signed February 23, 2011, but the assignment was not notarized until April 6, 2011. So we are arguing that Bank of America did not own the loan when they signed the notice of default. Thus they need to start over."

"Impressive," Alexis said. "Now, can you address my unaffordable mortgage issues?"

"Okay, let me break this down," I said.

"Go, Coach, speak the word," Alexis said.

"First, I will teach you how to wiggle," chimed in Emily. "You can play with your lender's head. Pretend like you are interested in a modification."

"But I *am* interested in a modification," Alexis said.

"Yes, but not the whack modification they're actually going to offer you," Emily said. "You won't get a good deal until you fight and buy lots of time. You need to be patient, right, Coach?"

"Yes, buy time and be patient," I said, pleased with the way Emily was running the show. "They may offer you a trial modification to see if they can squeeze a few payments out of you without committing to a permanent modification. Don't take the bait. Most trial modifications are not successfully converted to permanent modifications."

"It's kind of like running a marathon," Emily said, "except you are not actually trying to move forward in the process with the bank."

"And send in a QWR," I said.

"On QWR Day," Emily added.

"Then you wait for the response, gather all your documents, and the legal pleadings when you are served with the lawsuit," I said.

"Should I accept the service of the lawsuit?" Alexis asked.

"Well, you can duck and dodge a while," I said. "You can gain some additional time."

"Additional time is good," Emily said. "Time is the debtor's friend and the creditor's enemy."

"That's right, Emily," I said. "Eventually, though, you probably will get served with the foreclosure lawsuit."

"Okay," Alexis said.

"You can avoid service for a while," I said. "But if they cannot find you, they'll put a legal notice in the paper."

"So wait, everyone will know you are in foreclosure?" asked Emily aghast.

"No," I said. "The legal notices are buried at the back of the paper. No one reads them."

"Okay, phew," said Emily.

"Besides, I don't mind if the world knows I am in foreclosure," said Alexis, sounding defiant. "Everyone knows that the banks caused this mess by selling overpriced mortgages, which set everyone up to fail."

"So we the people shouldn't be embarrassed?" Emily said. "But the banks should?"

"Exactly," I said. "Eventually you and your attorney answer the lawsuit and let Ocwen know about some of the deficiencies you've uncovered. The foreclosure courts in Ohio are backed up, so this could take years."

"And I can live for free all that time?" Alexis asked.

"Kind of," I said. "You should put the money you would spend on your housing payment into a settlement wallet. Even if the amount is less than what your mortgage is, set aside that amount each month and don't spend it. You will need to use those funds to settle your mortgage, or for legal fees. You might need the money soon, so start putting it away now and don't touch it. Right, Emily?"

"Yes, don't spend it no matter what," said Emily. "Even

if you have a once-in-a-lifetime vacation opportunity with the family." Emily and I stared at each other.

"So the settlement wallet is not a real wallet," Alexis said. "Just get the money out of my hands and put in a place where I can't touch it so I don't splurge on some new clothes?"

"Yes," I said.

"I'll give it to my mom," Alexis said.

"Perfect. Just stick to the plan," Emily said. "Debt Cleanse really works."

"I got it," Alexis said. "I am totally ready to do this. Now I just hope eventually Ocwen sells my mortgage to AHP," said Alexis. "Have you ever bought Ocwen mortgages?"

Yes, I said, "but the possibility of what you're suggesting is remote," I said. "But anyone besides Ocwen will be an improvement."

"Why is the possibility remote?" asked Alexis.

"Because we can't choose the loans we purchase," I said. "Instead, banks and other mortgage holders offer us pools of loans to bid on. If your loan happened to be in a pool, then maybe we could buy your mortgage."

"Okay," said Alexis.

"I'm just saying that you shouldn't get your hopes up that AHP will be able to buy your loan," I said. Underwater mortgages total over $566 billion, which includes many of the $350 billion in delinquent mortgages. Only $13.1 billion were sold in 2012 and $34.7 billion in 2013, so a lot more defaulted debt needs to be freed. "But AHP will buy all we can. That said, we've already bought some Ocwen loans and I expect they will sell more due to their recent regulatory challenges."

"Go get 'em, Coach," said Alexis.

"Yes, Mr. Newbery, buy all the mortgages up at discounts," Emily said. "Borrowers will like dealing with AHP better."

"Thanks," I said. "But there are millions of distressed mortgages out there, so we need to share our strategies with other debt buyers in order to have a real impact. We need to show how all debt buyers can be part of the solution to the country's unaffordable debt problem, while still earning a reasonable profit."

"So what's the worst thing that can happen?" asked Alexis, refocusing the conversation back to her dilemma. "Assume I try to fight Ocwen, but they have all their documents in order, a good attorney, and are on their game?"

"The worst thing is that you will likely have some extra cash," I said. "You'd stay in your home for a long, long time. In the end, though, you may need to move."

"But they cannot just show up and kick me out, right?" Alexis asked.

"Right. You would receive ample notice," I said. "Assume Ocwen wins and the court gives them a judgment that empowers them to foreclose. Next they hold a foreclosure sale."

"Then I'd have to leave?" asked Alexis.

"No, they still need to wait for a court to confirm the sale and the sheriff to record the deed. Eventually, they may get title to the house," I said. "But you still have possession, just like a renter."

"They would then need to evict?" asked Alexis.

"Yes, similar to a tenant not paying rent," I said. "Even though the tenant isn't paying, the landlord still has to go through the court process, provide evidence that they own the property, prove the amount due, and that they have the documents and records to back this up."

"Sounds like *Debt Cleanse: Renter's Edition*," said Emily. "Renters could use these tactics to stay in their homes longer if they cannot afford to pay."

"It sounds like we would have at least a few weeks after the foreclosure sale," Alexis said.

"A few months, in most cases," I said. "You can fight the eviction just like you fought the foreclosure: find the deficiencies in the documents and legal pleadings and exploit."

"Do we get to wiggle some more?" asked Emily.

"Yes, they might send an agent to the door offering cash for keys," I said. "Maybe five hundred or a thousand dollars to help with moving expenses." Many lenders will offer cash to occupants in order to save the legal costs of eviction, to limit any vandalism by outgoing occupants, and to get the property on the market faster. However, occupants are under no obligation to hand over the keys.

The extra time in the home is often worth more than the cash-for-keys incentive offered.

"So we can pretend like we want to move," said Emily, "but keep putting off signing the cash-for-keys agreement, maybe saying we are getting estimates for moving costs. They might put off filing the eviction."

"Exactly," I said. "My star pupil."

"Then, maybe we are slow to return phone calls. Do a little wiggling with the agent?" said Emily.

"Even after foreclosure, you can get a lot of time," I said. "We had a home we foreclosed on in Buffalo, New York, in December 2013. The lockout did not occur until September 2014. The process took nine months. First, we had to wait for the deed to be recorded, and then we started eviction. The borrower did some wiggling and, by the time we looked up, ten months had passed."

"And all this time we could be putting cash away in our settlement wallets," said Alexis. "We can use it to settle the debts, or pay legal fees, or even to move at the last possible moment."

"Excellent," I said. "Another star student."

"Thanks, Coach Newbery," said Alexis, gushing.

"Alexis, didn't you have another question?" said Emily.

"Did I?" asked Alexis. "What other question did I have?"

"About still owing money even if the bank took your house," said Emily.

"Oh, yes, yes," said Alexis. "What about deficiency judgments?"

"What is a deficiency judgment?" asked Emily.

"These are typically judgments that creditors can pursue if they sell a home or other item securing a loan for less than the amount due," I said. "For instance, Emily owes about $600,000 on a home worth $450,000. If the bank sold at $450,000 and netted $425,000 from the sale, they could sue Emily for the $175,000 difference."

"That's messed up. The banks get the home plus make me pay them even more cash?" Emily said. "I don't think you mentioned that before."

"In California, deficiency judgments are very uncommon," I said. "Lenders cannot get them if they use non-judicial foreclosure. Even if they choose to foreclose through the courts, the law is written so that mortgage companies cannot generally get deficiency judgments if the loan was made to purchase the home or even to refinance the purchase loan."

"What about Ohio?" Alexis asked.

"Ohio allows deficiency judgments," I said. "Again, though, most lenders do not pursue."

"What happens if Ocwen tries to get one against me?" asked Alexis.

"Same strategy," I said. "Execute your plan. When you agree to any settlement, make sure that the agreement states that the lender will not pursue a deficiency judgment."

"What if there is no settlement?" asked Alexis, sounding worried.

"When you are exploiting deficiencies and fighting the foreclosure in court," I said, "you are also fighting the deficiency claim. If you are in court duking it out, the lender will often waive the deficiency claim to move the process along faster. Many deficiency claims are awarded because the homeowner did not even answer the lawsuit."

"Understood, Coach," said Alexis. "I feel a lot better."

"That's great," I said, laying the cash for our lunch on the table.

"Are you sure you don't want to stay for dessert?" Emily asked. "Not even cheesecake?"

"No, I'm done," I said. "Alexis, great to meet you. Emily, always a pleasure."

"Thanks, Coach," said Alexis.

"Thanks, Mr. Newbery," said Emily.

CHAPTER 3

CREDIT CARDS AT OLIVE GARDEN

"WHITE RABBITS!" I EXCLAIMED. THEY WERE THE first words out of my mouth on October 1, 2014.

"What time is it?" my wife asked, groggily.

"Five forty-five," I said, wide-awake. I often get up early on weekdays to get an early start on the day.

"Why, again, do you insist on saying 'white rabbits' first thing on the first day of every month?" she asked. "More importantly, why are you waking me up so early?"

"I get good luck all month," I said. "That's what my mother taught me."

"But," said Verria, "could you whisper it?"

"No, I need to say it out loud," I said. "I'm not sure if whispering counts. You should try it."

"You are all the luck I need," she said.

"Such a charmer," I smiled as I got out of bed. "Come on. We need to get ready for work."

"Sure," she said. Twenty minutes later, we were in the kitchen preparing our lunches.

"Are you going to have any of the soup?" I asked, eyeing the large container of garbanzo bean soup in the refrigerator. "I would like to take it for lunch."

"Ummm," she said.

"It wasn't that great this time," I added, hoping to dissuade her.

"I know it was good," she said. "But you can have it anyway. But leave me the grilled cauliflower."

"You want all the cauliflower?" I asked.

"Yes, I want all the cauliflower," she said. "There's not even that much left."

"Okay," I said. "I'll let you have it all. I feel lucky today."

"Okay, my white rabbit," she said. "Let's get going."

"I'm not white," I said. "I'm a Hispanic rabbit."

"Whatever, funnyman. Either way, you're my rabbit," she said. "But do you ever think that saying white rabbits is just a superstition?"

"Maybe, but saying it does not take much effort," I said. "Maybe just thinking you will have good luck is all you need." We made our way down to the lobby in our apartment building.

"But did you say white rabbits during the Woodland

Meadows' collapse?" asked Verria.

"Yes," I said. I knew where she was going with her questioning.

"That was an unlucky time for you," she said.

"I know," I said. "But maybe saying white rabbits made what happened better. Maybe it could have gone worse?"

"I can't imagine that period going any worse for you than it did," she said.

"I know," I said. We were now walking East on Roosevelt Road. There was a brisk wind blowing in off the lake. "But I met you during that time. Maybe that was because I kept saying white rabbits? Maybe you were my good fortune?" We walked silently for a minute. Verria was apparently pondering my response.

"I love you," she said, looking at me.

"I love you, too," I said. "And you really should try saying white rabbits."

"Did you say white rabbits that month you had the situation at Olive Garden?" she said.

"Did someone say Olive Garden?" asked a male voice. "I love Olive Garden." We both looked up and saw T. J., who was my personal trainer at our gym Fitness Formula Club for a couple of months in 2012. We had become friends. Now he worked for the City of Chicago, and we'd occasionally bump into him on the street.

"Good morning, T. J.," I said.

"Hi, T. J.," said Verria.

"What's up, Jorge," T. J. said. "Hi, Verria."

"Nice morning," I said.

"Yes, but a bit chilly," said T. J., who was African American, somewhere in his thirties, and just under six-feet tall with a muscular build. We were all walking together north on State Street toward downtown. "So what is the situation at Olive Garden?"

"Yes," I asked, looking at Verria. "What situation at Olive Garden?"

"You know," she said. "In Dayton."

"Oh that," I said, dreading the recollection.

"Tell T. J. the story," Verria said.

"Do you want me to give you the full story, even before we stepped foot in Olive Garden?" I asked. "It's sad, but funny too."

"Sure," T. J. said as we walked across Ninth Street. "Tasty as well, I bet."

"So, ten years ago, in 2004," I began, "I owned over four thousand apartments across the country, including the eleven-hundred unit Woodland Meadows in Columbus, Ohio."

"I've heard about Woodland Meadows," said T. J., sounding empathetic.

"So I traveled for business extensively," I said. "I mostly flew on Southwest Airlines, which back then had a generous rapid rewards program, great service, no change fees. To get more rapid rewards points, I was swiping my

Southwest Chase Bank credit card every chance I got."

"He would even charge a newspaper or a juice," Verria said.

"The more money I charged, the more points I racked up, and the more free tickets I earned," I said. "I paid off my five-thousand-dollar balance each month so that I could free up room to charge more."

"I do the same with my NFL card," said T. J. "So I can get jerseys and stuff like that."

"Well, I accrued so many points that I earned a companion pass, enabling me to take a companion with me on flights free for a year," I said. "I charged everything I could on that credit card."

"I thought the story was about Olive Garden," T. J. said.

"Olive Garden is coming," I said. "I started stumbling financially in 2005, and I was unable to pay all my bills."

"That was a tough time," said Verria. "Lots of bad luck."

"By 2006, I had to choose which bills to pay," I said. "But I always paid that Southwest card on time every month. I used it everywhere."

"I got jealous sometimes," Verria said. "I used to think, 'Who does this man love more, that Southwest card or me?'"

"I was just getting to know *you*," I said. Verria playfully punched my arm. "Ouch."

"By 2007, all your credit cards were shut down," Verria said. "Except that Southwest card. The Woodland Meadows fallout just devastated you financially."

"I even started carrying a balance each month," I said. "But I always paid at least the minimum payment and was never late."

"It was his payment priority," Verria said to T. J. "At times, he wasn't paying anything else except Southwest."

"I wasn't charging so much anymore," I said. "But I was still earning some points. And I had this fantasy that everything was going to turn around and return to normal."

"But it never did," Verria said.

"In the summer of 2007, I got a notice from Chase that my interest rate was being increased to almost thirty percent because of recent derogatory items on my credit report," I said. "Basically, since I wasn't paying others, I was considered a higher risk. This was known as universal default. It didn't seem fair."

"Yes, especially when raising the rate to thirty percent made it harder to pay," T. J. observed.

"Exactly," I said. "Here I was struggling to make the Southwest payments and then they make the interest rate and payment a whole lot higher, like they wanted me to fail."

"But you were determined," Verria said.

"Yes, I was going to keep us together," I said. "Me and Southwest."

"Sounds like you missed the signs," T. J. said. "They no longer wanted you."

"Yes, I missed all the hints," I said. "So when I got a decent commission check, I gave it all to Southwest. I wanted to demonstrate my commitment."

"He made a four-thousand-dollar payment, reducing the five-thousand-dollar balance to one thousand dollars," Verria said. "You seemed relieved."

"I was," I said. "I finally had some air to breathe. Then Olive Garden happened."

"Sounds ominous," T. J. said.

"A couple of days later, Verria and I were at Olive Garden in Dayton, Ohio," I said. "We were still courting."

"We had gone beyond courtship," Verria said.

"I ordered the never-ending soup, salad, and bread-sticks," I said. "I was so tired of that soup and salad, but I was on a budget."

"But he told me he really liked it, so I wouldn't know how rough things were going for him," Verria said. "He kept ordering more and more, just to get full."

"At six dollars and ninety-five cents, that was a cheap meal," I said. "But after we were done, I used the Southwest card to pay."

"But, the waitress came back and said she was having trouble processing the card," Verria said.

"I assured her that I had recently paid and asked her to run again," I said.

"But she came back again," Verria said. "And she said that she could not process."

"I was absolutely confident that I had available credit," I said. "So I called the eight hundred number on the back of the card and checked the available balance through the automated system. The message came on and said, 'You have no available credit'."

"Oh, man," T. J. said. "In front of your date."

"His eyes were bugged out like he was losing his mind," Verria said. "But he kept smiling at me and the waitress."

"How could this be? I kept thinking," I said. "So I pressed zero to talk to someone, and a high-pitched Indian voice answered. I verified my information and asked why I had no available credit when I had just paid four thousand dollars. She advised that my credit limit had been lowered to one thousand dollars due to reasons which would be explained in a letter."

"What's the reason?" I pressed. "She said they were not authorized to disclose the reason and that I had to wait for the frickin' letter. I was so frustrated."

"I had to pay for the meal," Verria said, giggling. "I kept thinking, what kind of relationship was I getting myself into?"

"Well, here you both are now," T. J. said. "Marital bliss."

"I don't know about bliss, but it's good," I said.

"It's bliss," Verria said. She punched me in the arm, hard this time.

"See you, T. J." I said, shaking his hand.

"Bye," said Verria.

"See you two later. We should get together for lunch one day," T. J. said.

"How about Olive Garden?" I said. We all shared a laugh. Verria and I continued the walk to work.

"Do you remember what happened after that day?" I asked.

"No," she said, her curiosity piqued. "What happened?"

As my credit score had dropped, Chase apparently wanted to close my account. However, if they did that, they likely assumed I would stop paying altogether. Considering that I had made the $4,000 payment with the intention of charging living expenses over the next couple of months, the credit limit reduction was a horrific setback at one of my lowest points. Nevertheless, Chase was not done with me yet.

"I was devastated about how Southwest treated me that day at Olive Garden," I said. "But I recovered. At some point, I came up with a thousand dollars and paid the remaining amount due on my card. I thought we still had a chance to keep going together."

"You are always so optimistic," she said.

"The next morning, I verified online that the payment was credited," I said. "Then I stopped for gas at the Speedway gas station off the Seventy-Five Freeway near the Miller Lane off ramp. But my card didn't work."

"You never told me this," said Verria.

"I was too embarrassed," I said. "I called Southwest

and asked what happened this time. I had been a loyal customer for several years and only had a thousand-dollar credit line. Surely, they were not going to cut me down any further."

"But they did?" she said.

"Yes, once again, a high-pitched Indian voice advised me that my card had been cancelled, and I would receive a letter," I said.

"You were probably furious," she said.

"Southwest took my last thousand dollars, and then they shut me down without warning," I said. "All I could think was, 'No way. You can't treat me like this. Not after all we've been through.'"

"What'd you do?" she asked.

"I drove to Fifth Third Bank and put a stop payment on that thousand-dollar payment," I answered. We started laughing.

"You got the last word in that time," she said.

"It was a tough time," I said. "I felt like I was drowning." If your credit is great, banks fall over themselves offering you credit cards. However, as soon as you run into trouble, credit card issuers can reduce your limit or cancel your card immediately without any notification.

We arrived at our building. As we exited the elevator, I asked Verria a question.

"Verria, do you have some time to join me on a call with Alexis?" I asked. "She texted me a couple of nights ago and wants to talk about her credit cards."

"Emily's friend?" she asked. "One of your star students?" She hadn't been thrilled with the idea of my lunch with two beautiful Latinas.

"Yes, Emily's friend," I said, feeling a tad guilty. "But you are my only star."

"Sure, what time?" she asked.

"Let's do it now," I said.

"Okay," said Verria, as we dropped our stuff in our respective offices.

"Hi, is this Alexis?" I asked. I was on the speakerphone in AHP's conference room with Verria.

"Yes, this is she," Alexis said.

"This is Jorge," I said. "You texted me a couple of nights ago. I also have my wife, Verria, here with me."

"Good morning, Jorge and Verria," Alexis said.

"Good morning, Alexis," Verria said firmly. "I just want to get one thing clear, Jorge and I are in marital bliss and I am his only star."

"Okay," said Alexis, sounding perplexed.

"Hold on, Alexis, give us just a few seconds," I said, taken aback by Verria's outburst. I put the phone on mute.

"You okay?" I asked.

"Yes, put her back on," Verria said. I unmuted the phone.

"Alexis, I apologize," Verria said. "I am really sorry. There was a bit of confusion over here. How can we help?"

"My credit cards are a real problem," Alexis said.

"Bigger than I thought. I can't keep paying them either."

"Alexis, yours is a familiar story in this country," I said. "The average US household credit card debt is $15,480."

"Well, I am above average in this respect," Alexis said. "I owe over $120,000."

"Dang," I heard Verria say under her breath. Alexis must have heard.

"I don't know how it got so high," Alexis said. "I don't buy luxuries or anything."

"What happened?" Verria asked. I try never to ask that. Some people like to share the blow-by-blow of how they got into their mess. To me, how they got into debt is unimportant. Where they are going from here is what I can help with. Verria, however, is the type who wants to know.

"I was a legal secretary for seventeen years at the same firm, making good money," Alexis said. "I thought I'd retire there. Then the recession hit and my ex was laid off. We divorced soon after that, and we spent our modest savings on legal fees to split up. I ended up with almost nothing but this house with no equity. Finally, to top it all off, last year I was laid off."

"Sorry to hear that," Verria said.

"Now, getting a decent job is difficult," Alexis said.

"The job market gets tougher as you get older," Verria said.

"I might have to move back in with my parents, but I'm divorced, and I have full custody of our three kids, so I don't want to overwhelm them," Alexis said. "But I feel overwhelmed."

"How are you surviving?" asked Verria.

"I pick up some temp work, which doesn't pay well and has no benefits. I do what I have to do," said Alexis. "I sporadically get child support from my ex. He's always running behind, a real scoundrel."

"You have been surviving off the credit cards?" asked Verria.

"Yes, and then I had a few late payments," Alexis said. "They jacked my interest rates up. I feel like I'm drowning."

I had heard enough. "Alexis, just stop paying everything," I said.

"What do you mean?" she asked.

"Alexis, you can stop paying all your unaffordable debt," I said. "Credit cards, car loans, student loans, payday loans, whatever you have."

"Really?" she asked.

"Yes, and then you work them the same as I told you to manage your mortgage," I said. "Exploit deficiencies and drag it out. Eventually, you can settle for big discounts or even nothing. Most of the creditors will eventually sell to debt buyers like AHP at big discounts," I said. "You can then usually make favorable deals to settle."

"But can't they garnish my wages, levy my bank account, and put a lien on my home?" Alexis asked.

"They could. But first they need to get a court judgment," I said. "And I'll show you how to prevent that."

"I need to understand what I am getting myself into," Alexis said. "Tell me how I prevent a judgment."

"After you stop paying, your creditors will call you incessantly," I said.

"Some of them already do," Alexis said.

"The goal is to withstand the collection efforts," I said. "Just ignore the calls, block the collectors' numbers, and file away the mail they send. If you do talk to them, log the time, the day, who you spoke to, and a summary of the call."

"I can do that," said Alexis, sounding determined.

"Then in maybe six months or a year, your creditors may start selling your debts," I said. "That's what you want." In a Federal Trade Commission study of the nine largest debt buyers in the United States representing more than 75 percent of the consumer debts sold in 2008, the organization found that over $143 billion in debt was sold for $6.5 billion. Sixty-two percent of this was credit card debt.

"Why do I want that?" Alexis asked.

"Alexis, you want your debts sold because they will be sold at big discounts," I said. "If you owe Bank of America five thousand dollars, then it might be sold for two hundred dollars—four percent of what you owe." The FTC concluded that, based on an analysis of prices paid by debt buyers in more than thirty-four hundred portfolios, debt buyers paid an average of four cents per dollar of debt face value.

"Wow," Alexis said. "I didn't know they sold at such big discounts. Maybe I could offer them five hundred dollars, and they make a profit and we all move on."

"That's how it should work," I said. "Unfortunately, most debt buyers will try to collect the full amount owed and threaten you with wage garnishment, bank levies, and other aggressive tactics."

"That's what I am afraid of," Alexis said, sounding deflated.

"But the longer you go without paying," I said, "the more likely your debt will be resold again to another debt buyer at an even bigger discount. The longer you can go without paying, the more likely you can settle at greater discounts." The FTC report observed that older debt sold for a significantly lower price than newer debt.

"What happens when they get sold?" asked Alexis.

"When they sell those debts, they'll usually send you an invitation to dispute the debt," I said.

"Invitations. Ha!" Alexis said. "But I owe the money. What am I disputing?"

"That's not the point," I said. "The FTC study reported that debt buyers did not have the data and documents to verify almost half of the disputed debts. The report revealed that debt buyers often could not verify the total due; breakdown what they demanded into principal, interest, and charges; prove that they owned the debt; or even provide evidence that a debt existed."

"Excellent. I'll do the disputes," Alexis said. "Is there a form?" If every consumer disputed the debts acquired by debt buyers in 2008, then by extrapolating the FTC's findings, almost $70 billion of the $143 billion sold to debt buyers could not be verified.

"I will e-mail you a link to one on DebtCleanse.com after this call."

"Great," said Alexis. "Thanks." She continued, "I still can't get over my debts being sold for four percent. That means my one-hundred-and-twenty thousand-dollar debt could be sold for forty-eight hundred dollars. I pay over twenty-five hundred dollars a month just on the minimum payments, so that is like two months of payments."

"I agree, it's crazy," I said. "If you owe five thousand dollars on your credit card with an interest rate of eighteen percent, and you pay a minimum payment of two percent of the outstanding balance, then paying off that debt will take over forty-six years."

"I don't even know if I'll live another forty-six years," Alexis said. "And if I do, I don't want to be slaving away paying off credit card debts all that time. That's one and a half times as long as a thirty-year mortgage."

"Yes, if you are over thirty-three and you live the average American lifespan of seventy-eight years," I said. "Do not expect the minimum payments to pay off your five-thousand-dollar credit card debt before you die."

"Dang," Verria and Alexis said at the same time.

"So don't pay," I said. "Instead, each month, put the payments you were scheduled to pay into your settlement wallet."

"Got it," Alexis said. "So what happens after I dispute the debts?"

"The odds are about fifty-fifty that the debt buyer can verify your debt," I said. "If your debt cannot be verified, the debt will likely die."

"Die?" asked Alexis.

"Yes," I said. "As in, you pay zero. That FTC report found that once a debt is disputed and the debt buyer is unable to verify in response to dispute letters, less than one percent of that debt is sold to other debt buyers. They just write it off."

"Poof?" Alexis asked.

"Yes, poof," I said. "The Fair Debt Consumer Protection Act prohibits debt collectors, including debt buyers, from seeking to recover on unverified disputed debt."

"Awesome," said Alexis.

"Unfortunately, it does not bar them from reselling such debts to other purchasers, or bar subsequent purchasers from seeking to collect the debt," I said. "Still, even if disputed debt is verified, less than five percent of verified disputed debts are resold."

"Why can't they verify these debts?" Alexis asked.

"The FTC report identified that, for most portfolios, debt buyers did not receive any documents at the time of purchase," I said. "Instead, debt buyers were typically given anywhere from six months to three years to request documents on up to ten to twenty-five percent of the files at no charge."

"Scoundrels," Alexis said. "They are trying to collect on debts when they don't even have the documents and records to back it up? Is that even legal?"

"Apparently, this is legal," I said, "But if you push back, then they will likely drop the collection efforts if they can't validate. You can even make the debt buyer pay the debt seller to try to get your documents."

"How?" Alexis asked.

"If their requests exceeded the ten to twenty-five percent allowed, then the debt buyer has to pay to get documents, usually between five and ten dollars per document," I said. "Debt sellers usually have substantial time, like thirty to sixty days, to respond to requests for documents. There is no guarantee that the seller can even find the documents."

"That is outrageous," said Alexis.

"Yes, it is," I said. "All the debt buyers typically receive is a bit of electronic data showing the name, address, social security number, account number, and a dollar amount supposedly due."

"They are called tapes," Verria said. "We get these at

AHP when we buy loans."

"Okay, but what if they *can* verify my debt," Alexis said. "What happens then?"

"They might sue you," I said. "But you have rights just like the creditor does. And by disputing the debt, the debt buyer knows that you are ready for a fight. Thus a significantly discounted settlement might become attractive."

"Say they don't want to settle, though" said Alexis.

"They can choose not to settle, just like you can choose not to pay," I said. "However, they need to start spending legal fees to go to court and prove that you owe them the amount they claim."

"And that they have the documents and records to back it up," Verria said.

"My star," I said. Verria smiled at me warmly.

Just then we could hear Alexis break down a bit through the phone. "Oh, Alexis" Verria said. "Everything will be okay. We'll try and help."

"You can only take so much, you know?" Alexis said.

"I hear you," said Verria.

"Yeah," Alexis said. "Life's rough out here."

"Life's rough all over," said Verria.

"I try to keep everything normal for my kids, you know," said Alexis.

"I bet," said Verria.

"Dance lessons, sports teams, school trips," Alexis said. "I have trouble saying no to them. I want them to have all the opportunities and experiences they want. I'd do anything for them, but the expenses are really eating into my funds, you know?"

"You sound like a great mom," said Verria.

I switched on my laptop and checked e-mails, as the back and forth appeared to have turned into more of a female conversation.

"But I need cash to survive, you know," said Alexis.

"I hear you," said Verria.

"I could only get so many temp jobs, as the market here in Cleveland is so weak. They keep talking about how the economy is improving and unemployment is going down, but I don't see it," said Alexis. "Neither do my friends and family. Everyone is still struggling. Nothing seems to be getting any better."

"Yes, I hear the same all over this country," said Verria. "Everyone feels left behind. The only ones recovering appear to be the rich."

"I even got some payday loans, but I couldn't get much because my hours go up and down," said Alexis. "Then I hit rock bottom."

"Rock bottom?" asked Verria.

"Yes, rock bottom," said Alexis.

"What happened?" asked Verria.

"Craigslist," said Alexis.

"Craigslist?" asked Verria.

"I put an ad on Craigslist," said Alexis.

"An ad for what?" asked Verria.

"Casual encounters," confessed Alexis, sounding relieved as she revealed a big pent-up secret that had clearly been gnawing away at her. The "Casual Encounters" section of Craigslist is often used for prostitution. I looked up from my e-mail box and turned my head toward Verria. Our eyes met. She looked sad.

"Wow, Alexis, things must have been bad," said Verria.

"I didn't know where else to turn," said Alexis. "My ex is not helpful, always late on his child support. My family is in the same straits as me. I had even borrowed from my oldest daughter. She is sixteen and took a summer job, and I borrowed what she had saved. I felt terrible," said Alexis, choking up again.

Alexis is not alone: 30 percent of parents have borrowed from their children.

"You did what you thought was best for your kids," said Verria.

Prostituting yourself is best for your children? I thought to myself. I guess she felt there was no other choice.

"I did it for them," said Alexis.

"How much did you get paid?" asked Verria. I looked over at her like maybe we shouldn't be asking questions like that.

"I asked two hundred and fifty dollars for an hour, and I'd do whatever they wanted," Alexis said. "Most of them tipped like thirty or fifty dollars. The money was good."

"Wow," said Verria. I didn't know what to say, so I stayed quiet. I don't think Verria knew what else to say, either.

"Oh, Alexis," I finally mustered. "I am so sorry to hear that your unaffordable debt forced you to these extremes."

"I am sorry," Alexis said. "I didn't mean to share all my troubles with you. I wish I could sue the banks for putting me through all this."

"Well, they may sue you first," I said, relieved to change the subject away from such a dark issue, "trying to collect."

"I really didn't mean to share all my challenges with you," Alexis said coolly, as if she had just refocused. "So what do I do when they sue me?"

"If they sue you in small claims, you show up in person," I said, "without an attorney."

"What do I say?" asked Alexis.

"In court, the judge will likely ask each side to state their claim," I said. "Just relax and state your claims and requests calmly and in a relaxed manner."

"I can do calm," said Alexis.

"The debt buyer will say that you owe the money," I said.

"Then I say that I don't owe the money," said Alexis.

"Basically, yes," I said. "Just deny the debt."

"Wouldn't denying the debt be lying?" asked Alexis.

"No. For instance, you may be asked whether you owe $5,821 or whatever the figure is," I said. "You can state that you do not know what, if anything, is due and that you would like a payment history and a breakdown of the alleged debt by principal, interest, and charges in order to help determine what, if anything, is due. The judge will likely ask you and the creditor to convene in the hallway to try to work something out on your own."

"Is that when I try to settle?" asked Alexis.

"Maybe," I said. "When you're in the hallway, if you want to get this behind you, offer a settlement of five percent of what you owe and see how they respond. The representative for the opposition is generally just as eager to get this behind them as you are, so they may work something out. However, don't feel pressured. Be willing to go back in front of the judge repeating your requests if needed. The debt buyer is unlikely to possess the documents you are asking for. Thus they should not be able to win a judgment against you."

"Sounds like a plan," Alexis said. "What happens if this is in regular court?

"You must answer the lawsuit," I said.

"What do I put in my answer?" Alexis asked.

"Take a look at the lawsuit you were served with, which will have been prepared by the creditor's attorney," I said. "Is there a contract attached? Typically, there's just a brochure or boilerplate card member agreement without anything specifically identifying you. Look for anything with your signature. Chances are there is nothing you signed in the whole stack. Also, check to see if the contract even names the correct original creditor."

"I can put my legal skills to work," Alexis said.

"Yes, you'll feel like Columbo," I said. "Then ask for a jury trial. In the unlikely event that your case *does* go to court, then a jury of your peers will decide the fate of your debt. As most Americans are also victims of the banks, the specter of a jury trial makes pushing the case forward even less attractive for creditors."

"Got it," said Alexis. "What else?"

"One more thing," I said. "Repeatedly, these creditors try to cover-up their shortcomings by providing an affidavit to the court. An employee for the creditor signs a template document stating the date you allegedly opened the account and how much you purportedly owe. This is supposedly based on a review of the creditor's records. The document is then often notarized in order to provide an official look."

"Sounds imposing," said Alexis.

"Don't be fooled," I said. "Let the court know that you want copies of the books and records the signer of the affidavit reviewed. Most of the times, the signer didn't review anything and is simply robo-signing these affidavits all day."

"I should be taking them to court," Alexis said.

"Whether you end up in small claims or regular court, you'll be looking for deficiencies and errors to exploit," I said. "You can dispute the amount they claim is due and whether the plaintiff—the company suing you—even owns the debt. You can ask for documentation as to the debt, such as the credit card agreement you signed, an assignment of the debt from the original creditor to the debt buyer, an accounting of all payments made for the debt buyer to prove that you owe the money, and a summary of what is principal, interest, and charges."

"Sounds like everything I would have asked for in the dispute letter," said Alexis. "What if they already provided all this in response to my dispute letter?"

"Ask for everything again," I said. "Chances are that they are missing something. Most debtors assume that they owe the money and will lose in court, so they don't even show up and the creditors win. Thus, be the exception and show up."

"Phew, okay," said Alexis.

"Court can be nerve-racking for anyone," I said.

"Can't be any more dreadful than meeting some creepy guy off Craigslist," said Alexis. "What other mistakes can I look for?"

"Let's see," I said. "Check to see if the interest rate is the same in the agreement, the lawsuit, and any agreement they provide. See if all their dates match: Does the day you signed the purported agreement, if any, match the date in the lawsuit?"

"Isn't there a statute of limitations?" asked Verria.

"Yes," I said. "The date of default, which is the date

you stopped paying, determines when the statute of limitations begins to run. If the creditor can produce a written contract that you signed when you first opened the account, then they have ten years to collect. If verbal or, if the written contract was modified without your signature acknowledgment, then they have five years to collect."

"What happens if I didn't pay for a couple of months, then I made a payment?" asked Alexis.

"Generally, making any payment restarts the statute of limitations," I said.

"So better not to pay even a token amount?" asked Alexis. "Unless I am fully settling the debt?"

"My star student," I said. Verria caught my eye with a stern look.

"Hey, Alexis," said Verria.

"Yes?" Alexis asked.

"Have you ever heard the expression 'White rabbits?'" asked Verria.

"Yes, Susan, my five-year old," said Alexis. "She says it first thing on the first day of every month. I heard her say it this morning." I started chuckling. Verria was quizzically grinning.

"What's funny?" asked Alexis.

"Jorge says it first thing on the first of every month as well," said Verria. "He thinks it brings good luck. But he's a bit older than five."

"My ex does the same thing," Alexis said. "His grandparents grew up in England around the time of World War Two and he said that the fighter pilots used to say it to stay safe in combat."

"My mom grew up in England during World War Two as well," I said. "She's the one who taught me."

"My ex said it every month religiously, especially as our finances and marriage were disintegrating. He was hoping for a better outcome, some lucky break," Alexis said. "I miss him. He taught all the kids to say it, but I think only Susan still does."

"Maybe I will start saying white rabbits," said Verria. We smiled at each other.

"I love you," I silently mouthed to Verria.

"I love you, too," Verria silently mouthed back.

"I didn't say white rabbits today," said Alexis. "But this call is my good luck for the month. I feel a lot better. Thanks to both of you."

"You are welcome, Alexis," I said.

"Bye," said Verria. We hung up the line.

---- CHAPTER 4 ----

PAYDAY LOANS: CALL ME 911

"HAPPY BIRTHDAY," SAID MY WIFE ON TUESDAY, October 21, 2014.

"It's not my birthday," I said.

"But it will be in eight days," she said. "What do you want for your special day?"

"Peace, happiness, you," I said, not really focusing. I was shaving. My wife was sorting through a large chest we have, putting away summer clothes, and bringing out the winter gear. We had been up since 6:00AM and needed to head to work soon.

"Really, what do you want?" she asked.

"I don't know. We can go to dinner at Native Foods," I said. "Maybe take a walk by the lake if the weather is nice. I'll be forty-nine. I'm not sure if I should be celebrating."

"You'll be fifty next year," she said.

"Oh joy," I said, with mock happiness. "My golden years."

"*Our* golden years," she said, correcting me.

"Get me a portable steamer," I said.

"A what?" she said.

"You know, like a steamer to unwrinkle clothes," I said, "but a portable one. My clothes always get crinkled when I travel. You can probably buy one on eBay."

"A steamer seems so practical," she said. "So unromantic."

"The romance comes from spending time with you," I said.

"Okay, Mr. Romance, I'll try to find a steamer on eBay," she said.

"Pay for it in cash," I said. "Don't use Bill Me Later."

"Okay, funnyman," she said. "They probably cost around fifty dollars, so I think I can swing that all cash. No financing necessary."

"But what if the steamer comes with an extended warranty?" I said, persisting. "That might add quite a bit to the price."

"I do not buy extended warranties," she said. "They are very overpriced, and the protection they offer is nominal. They are not a wise investment."

"Your answer is correct," I said, teasingly. "Let's get going."

We walked to the office. The weather was wet, windy, and generally dreary. Drainage in downtown Chicago is poor in many spots and there were puddles everywhere.

On that morning, we felt like we were navigating a swamp. We didn't speak a word. Instead, we focused on completing our voyage as quickly, comfortably, and dryly as possible. However, the peace ended as soon as we arrived at work.

"CALL ME 911 ASAP 716-476-1489," read the text that appeared on my cell as I walked into my office. I took off my jacket and hung it on the back of my office door. Then I sat down and called the number.

"Hello," a female voice said, sounding frantic.

"This is Jorge Newbery," I said. "I am returning a call to this number."

"Mr. Newbery, it's Alexis," she said. "Emily's friend."

"Oh hi, Alexis," I said. "How are you?"

"Bad, real bad," she said gravely. "I got picked up."

"Picked up?" I asked.

"By the police," she said. "For solicitation," she whispered.

"Oh, I am so sorry to hear that," I said.

"Yes, they responded to my Craigslist ad," she said. "I think it was entrapment."

"I don't know those laws very well," I said. "Have you gotten an attorney?"

"No," she said. "I'm in the holding area being processed. They want me to post bail."

"Okay," I said, as I turned on my computer.

"You are the only person I contacted," she said. "You need to get me out of here."

"Well, I am in Chicago and you are in Cleveland," I said, thinking of my calendar full of my own challenges that morning. I wasn't really in a position to add another one. "Isn't there someone else you can call?"

"You and Verria are the only two people I ever told about what I do on Craigslist," she said. "No one else knows. I can't call my family or friends."

"Let me think," I said.

"You need to get me out of here now," she said, sounding almost hysterical. "I need to get home to my children. They are going to be home this afternoon and wonder where I am."

"Hold on," I said. I got up and walked to Verria's office. "Verria," I said. "Do you have a minute?"

"Sure," she said.

"In my office," I said. "I have Alexis on the phone. She's in a jam." Once Verria walked in, I closed my office door.

"Hi, Alexis," I said, clicking the speakerphone on. "Verria is here, too." Verria sat down in one of the two chairs facing my desk.

"Hi, Verria," Alexis said.

"Hi, Alexis," Verria said. "What's going on?"

"I got picked up for solicitation," Alexis said. "I need you guys to get me out of here, now!"

"Craigslist?" Verria asked.

"Yes," Alexis said. "Some troll cop entrapped me."

"How much is bail?" Verria asked.

"Five hundred dollars," said Alexis.

"Okay," said Verria, who looked at me with an air of frustration.

"They take credit cards," Alexis added helpfully. "I can pay you back."

"Hold on," Verria said, as she muted the call.

"Look, Alexis sounds like a nice lady, and I realize that she has been through some tough times," Verria said. "I feel for her, I really do. But we barely know her. Let's not make her problem our problem."

"I agree," I said. "But think of her kids wondering where she is when they get home. Think of her family finding out what she's been doing to survive. This is a terrible predicament for her. Not just now, but her husband left her, she got laid off, she's been hooking up with creeps on Craigslist. All this because of unaffordable debt. Besides, it's five hundred dollars. It's not that much."

"But you told her to stop paying everything," said Verria, clearly exasperated. "Why is she still working on Craigslist?"

"I am sure she will pay us back," I said.

"You basically told her to stiff everyone," said Verria. "What makes you think she is going to pay us? We aren't going to have any documents, and we'll probably just have a whole lot of deficiencies. We'll never collect."

"Make it my birthday present," I said. "Maybe it comes back, maybe it doesn't. I think it will."

"Listen to yourself," Verria said. "You want us to pay five hundred dollars to bail out a lady arrested because she was prostituting herself on Craigslist. That birthday present is not romantic, or even practical."

"Five hundred dollars would make a huge difference to Alexis," I said. "We'll have a good feeling about helping her."

"I have a bad feeling already," Verria said. "We're not exactly rolling in dough, you know. We were married over two years ago and still no honeymoon."

"But I said we will go to Puerto Rico over Christmas and New Year's," I said.

"But we haven't even bought the tickets yet," Verria said, "because cash is still tight ever since Woodland Meadows. I've been patient, real patient. I support you in everything you do, but sometimes you try to help others to your own detriment—*our* own detriment. You are my hero, but you can't be everyone's hero." Verria looked upset and dismayed, which is rare. I felt bad.

"We need to click Alexis back in," I said, releasing the mute button. "Alexis?"

"Yes," Alexis said. "I'm here."

"Two questions," I said. "First, did you stop paying everything?"

"Yes," Alexis said.

"Second, why did you keep working on Craigslist?" I asked.

"I needed to pay off the payday loans," she said.

"But I thought you just said you stopped paying everything," I said.

"I did," Alexis said. Verria gave me a look that said, "Is this girl on crack?"

"But you just said you are paying payday loans," I said, attempting to emphasize the confusion in my voice.

"The payday loans aren't payments," Alexis said. "When I took the loans, I gave the payday lenders checks or electronic authorizations to get repaid from my bank accounts. I am trying to get those covered. That's why I am still working on Craigslist."

"Alexis," I said, dismayed. "You don't have to pay the payday loans."

"How?"

"Just close the bank accounts," I said, sitting back in my chair and looking at the ceiling. "Let those payments bounce."

"Isn't that illegal?" asked Alexis. "Like writing a bad check?"

"No, not at all," I said. "You can't take a loan knowing that you are going to close the account. That would be fraud."

"Okay," said Alexis, sounding unsure.

"But if you take out a payday loan today," I said, "and tomorrow you decide that you cannot pay or don't want to pay, then you can close the account. Let the payments bounce. Nothing illegal about that."

"How much do you have in payday loans?" asked Verria.

"About three thousand," Alexis said.

"How did you get so many?" I asked. The average payday loan is $350 and rarely do they reach over $1,000. Thus $3,000 is an awful lot of payday loans.

"You can get them from different lenders, online from Indian tribes. You just change your information around a bit." Alexis said. "It's easy to get the loans."

"How did you get up to three thousand dollars, though?" asked Verria.

"I got payday loans based on my temp job, my unemployment benefits, my kid's SSI," Alexis said. Although the name "payday loans" implies that borrowers need to have jobs, this is not the case. Many lenders will issue payday loans to be repaid by unemployment, disability, Social Security, and other recurring payments that are directly deposited into borrowers' bank accounts.

"There is little, if any, qualifying to ensure that borrowers can repay the loans," I said. "The vast majority of borrowers cannot both repay the loan and cover all their basic living expenses until their next payday."

Payday loans are not underwritten based on borrowers' ability to afford the loan, but rather rely on borrowers' *inability* to afford the payments and their need to borrow again and again. To entice new borrowers into destitution, payday lenders sometimes offer the first payday loan for free, no interest and no fees. The lender knows that there is a high likelihood that the borrower will be unable to repay the "free" loan and will become ensnared in months and even years of high borrowing costs. This is no different than a crack dealer who gives a free sample to try to get someone hooked on the drug, knowing they will have to come back again and again once addicted.

In fact, the targets of payday lenders and crack dealers fit similar profiles. A study by The Pew Charitable Trusts found that the most likely payday loan borrowers fit into one of five groups: those without a four-year college degree, home renters, African-Americans, those earning below $40,000 annually, and those who are separated or divorced. Alexis fit three of the five.

"For every one hundred dollars I borrow, I pay fifteen dollars to a payday lender," said Alexis. "So I get in a pinch and need three hundred and fifty dollars. I can pay back the payday lender four hundred dollars in two weeks. The cost is about fifty dollars, no big deal. I mean, I get fifty dollar tips sometimes."

"That's probably around four hundred percent APR," I said, after plugging the numbers into my calculator. "The APR is meaningless, though, if you don't pay off the debt in time."

"That's been my problem," said Alexis. "At the end of two weeks, I don't have the money to pay the loan back."

"So you get another loan?" I asked.

"Yes, every two weeks, I get new loans to pay off the old loans, paying another fifteen dollars per one hundred dollars to do so," Alexis said. "It's a trap I can't get out of. I keep getting deeper."

"Payday loans create a debt treadmill that makes struggling families worse off than they were before they received a payday loan," I said.

"I get so nervous that they'll come to my house if I don't pay," said Alexis. "I feel guilty buying food. I feel guilty when I fill my gas tank. I feel guilty paying anything, as I keep thinking that my money should all go to the payday lenders to get rid of them."

"You shouldn't feel guilty," said Verria, sounding shaken by Alexis' revelations.

"They are so easy to get," said Alexis.

"It's easy to not pay them as well," I said. "Please go and close all those accounts."

"But what happens then?" Alexis asked.

"Same as credit cards and other debt," I said. "The payday lender will call incessantly. You ignore them. Eventually, they'll probably sell the loans to some debt buyers at big discounts. You can dispute, demand documents and records. Same game."

"And none of the loans are over one thousand dollars," Alexis said, starting to sound relieved. "So they're too small for the creditors to justify litigating?"

"Exactly," I said. "You can settle these for pennies, or

even nothing."

"Why didn't you tell me this before?" Alexis asked.

"I told you to stop paying everything, which is what I tell everyone with unaffordable debts," I said. "Maybe I need to be more explicit on payday loans. I guess some people may not realize that the same tactics apply even if they have already given payday lenders postdated checks or authorizations."

"I will go and close the accounts," Alexis said. "But I need your help first to get me out of here."

"How much do you have in your bank account right now?" I asked.

"I don't know," Alexis said, pausing. "Maybe eight hundred dollars. But I wrote a check for twelve hundred dollars to a payday lender to clear on October 31 when I get paid by the temp agency."

"That's ten days away," I said. "The temp agency direct deposits your pay into that account?"

"Yes," said Alexis.

"Ask the temp agency to cancel the direct deposit permanently," I said. "Then open another account at a different bank and use that for direct deposits."

"I can do that," said Alexis.

"Do you know your bank account and routing numbers?" I asked.

"I do," Alexis said. "Let me get them from my phone."

"Okay," I said. Alexis provided her bank information.

"Verria, you got all that?" I asked.

"Got it," Verria said.

"Can you get me out of here?" said Alexis. "Give me freedom, please."

"Here's what we are going to do," I said. "If you say okay, we are going to initiate a five-hundred-dollar electronic debit from your bank account to hit tomorrow, that's October 22."

"Okay," said Alexis.

"Verria is going to use AHP's debit card to pay your bail," I said. "But, we'll get paid back tomorrow. You okay with that, Verria?"

"Sounds reasonable," said Verria.

"You okay with that, Alexis?" I asked.

"Yes. I really appreciate this," said Alexis. "I truly do."

"There's a bit more for you to do, Alexis," I said.

"Of course," Alexis said. "Anything."

"These are in addition to closing your bank accounts so the payday loan checks and debits bounce," I said.

"Okay," Alexis said.

"Stop taking out payday loans," I said.

"Got that," said Alexis.

"Google each of your payday lenders and add 'class action lawsuit' to the end," I said. "Many of the payday lenders are being sued in class actions, so you may as well join the classes. You might get your loan forgiven, and they even may pay you a settlement."

"I didn't know about that," said Alexis. "I can join the class actions for free, right?"

"Yes, you join free," I said. "But don't expect any huge windfall, as most goes to the attorneys, but these can help."

"For sure," said Alexis. "I'll join any and all class actions." In March 2014, a company doing business as Loan Point USA agreed to forgive the payday loans of 406 borrowers plus pay a $233,000 settlement, which included $60,000 for legal fees and the cost of locating borrowers and mailing checks. The checks went to borrowers who had already repaid their loans.

"And stop working Craigslist," I said. "I can kind of understand why you did this when you had no money, and you were trying to support your family. I get that."

"I know," Alexis said.

"But I have given you a plan," I said. "You can stop paying your unaffordable debts. I realize you still have life expenses, so you still need money."

"I know," Alexis said.

"But you have some temp work, unemployment, SSI, maybe a little child support," I said. "And there are regular jobs listed in Craigslist. AHP has hired most of our staff from there."

"But not from the 'Casual Encounters' section," said Verria. I stifled a laugh.

"Are you agreeable with all this, Alexis?" I asked.

"I am," said Alexis. We could hear Alexis sniffling

through the phone. Verria and I looked at each other, unsure what to say.

"Alexis, are you okay?" asked Verria.

"I'm okay," Alexis said. "I just really appreciate you guys. You hardly know me, but you are helping me out."

"We got to look out for each other," Verria said.

"We're all in this together," I said. "Alexis, I am going to transfer you to Verria's line so you can give her the instructions to pay the bail," I said. I smiled at Verria. She smiled back. Ten minutes later, Verria returned to my office.

"Alexis is sprung," she said.

"Nice," I said. "That felt good helping her out."

"I concur," said Verria. "I feel good, too."

"An early birthday present," I said.

"Well, I already ordered you the steamer on eBay," said Verria. "So you're getting that as well—only forty-six dollars and no extended warranty. No financing or payday loan required."

"Thanks," I said. Verria looked around to make sure no employees were looking. Then she leaned over, gave me a kiss on the cheek, and whispered in my ear:

"Happy birthday, hero."

CHAPTER 5

JOEY AND THE COPIER

"WE ARE HERE TO PICK UP THE COPIER." I HEARD a man's voice behind me. I was in Woodland Meadows' front office. My back was turned to the voice, as I was making copies on the very copier they were requesting. I knew why they were there. The finance company had been threatening to repossess Woodland Meadows' copier for weeks, as we were three months delinquent on our payments. The copier payment had seemed like a low priority, but the day of reckoning was now here.

"Can I help you?" I politely asked as I turned around. There were two men in work uniforms with name tags. The shorter man's said "Joey." His partner was "Tom."

"We were sent by the finance company to pick up the copier," said Joey. My mind had started racing for a solution. We needed the copier to copy leases, IDs, work orders, payments. This was before scanning was commonplace. Losing the copier would have brought our operation to a halt.

"There must be a mistake. We didn't request pick up," I said. There were several employees within earshot, and I expected that they were listening keenly.

"I can give you the number if you want to call," replied Joey, being helpful with a hint of impatience. This was late 2005, almost a year after the ice storm that had devastated the complex. The employees knew Woodland Meadows was in trouble, but I tried to keep everyone encouraged.

"Yes, let me do that," I replied to Joey. I expected that the employees were thinking, "Today, Woodland Meadows lets their copier go. Tomorrow, they let us go." I looked over at maintenance man Gavin sorting through work orders on his desk. His face looked solemn. A few years prior, he was a major drug dealer who was arrested for murder. He was released on a technicality, and even though word on the street was that he was guilty, he was making the best of his second chance. Outside of Woodland Meadows, his opportunities to earn a noncriminal living were limited. I glanced at Tonya, a former stripper who was now a leasing agent. Her face was stone cold and her body slumped. Gavin and Tonya and everyone working at Woodland Meadows had been let down by life before. I couldn't let them down. We needed to keep the copier.

"Yes, I am calling from Woodland Meadows, account

#3312COLU, and there are two gentlemen here to pick up our copier. I am trying to figure out what is going on," I said. I was put on hold after being advised that I was being transferred to a supervisor. I looked up and gave a broad grin to Joey, signaling that I was sure all this confusion would be worked out shortly. In reality, however, I wasn't sure how I was going to fix things.

I took several steps back to try to get out of the earshot of Joey, but stayed close enough that I could keep an eye on the copier in case he and his accomplice made any moves.

"Hi, your balance is thirteen hundred and fifty-one dollars, and we need payment in full. Otherwise, we need to repossess the copier," said the supervisor. "We can take a check by phone," he added in an optimistic tone. I was tempted to give them our bank account info to put out the fire. However, I knew that we did not have the money in our account. Even though I expected some rents in soon, we had more pressing needs like payroll and utility shut off notices.

"Can you take five hundred dollars?" I asked. I figured I could swing that and buy some time.

"No, we need the full thirteen hundred and fifty-one dollars," said the supervisor.

"We just don't have that now. I can only do five hundred dollars," I said.

"Then we need to proceed with repossession," said the supervisor. I started thinking to myself: this is a used copier. How much is it really worth? Plus, even though Joey and his sidekick could see the copier, we were on private property. They shouldn't be able to take the copier, I reasoned. I was unsure if I was correct.

"I can give you five hundred dollars now and five hundred dollars in thirty days. That's the best I can do," I said.

"No can do," said the supervisor. I hung up.

"You can't take the copier," I told Joey. My voice usually goes up a few pitches when I get confrontational, which is rare. I tried to say the words slow and deep, but they still came out an octave or two high.

"Let me call the finance company," Joey said. He walked downstairs, leaving his bouncer-looking partner behind. Joey's associate was imposing and burly, and he kept cracking his knuckles. As I looked at him, he seemed to be doing this mindlessly, but I wasn't sure if he was trying to be intimidating.

If you want to scrap, you need to look around, I thought to myself. We had a motivated and loyal office staff, but the combined rap sheet for this team would be both loaded and chilling. I looked at Big Mike, who was processing a delivery of maintenance supplies and was keeping watch over the proceedings. He had spent time in juvenile detention for strong-arm robbery.

"Let's go," Joey told his muscle when he came back upstairs. They left. I felt the flush of victory, however minor. More importantly, I took a stand in front of our employees and showed that we might be able to get through this period of strife. I returned to making my copies.

Joey and Tom had the right to ask us to voluntarily give up the collateral, in this case the copier, even though their phrasing was "we are here to pick up," which implied that they had the right to repossess regardless of whether we consented. However, since the copier was on private property, we had the right to refuse. The finance company's next step could have been to go to court to get an order to repossess. If they pressed the matter in court, we would have had the opportunity to challenge based on insufficient documentation, improper amount claimed as owed, deficiencies in documents and filings, and similar Debt Cleanse tactics. However, the finance company must have determined that the copier value was insufficient to warrant going to court. We never heard from the finance company again, never made another payment, and kept the copier.

Whether an auto, boat, Jet Ski, or any type of personal or business equipment, the same generally holds true: if the collateral is on private property and in a secured area, such as in a home or a locked garage or Woodland Meadows' office, creditors cannot repossess without the borrower's permission or a court order. Similar to Woodland Meadows' copier, the cost of going to court needs to be outweighed sufficiently by the value of the collateral. Otherwise, the creditor will likely cease repossession efforts and become agreeable to a discounted settlement offer. Alternately, you might just keep the collateral and never pay.

When Woodland Meadows closed, I took that copier to a complex I owned in Dayton and kept using it for a couple more years. Eventually, the copier broke down and the cost to repair it exceeded the value. Then I finally called back the finance company: "You can pick up the copier now."

CHAPTER 6

STUDENT LOANS AT JERRY'S DELI

"I'M IN A PREDICAMENT," SAID MY YOUNGEST brother Charles by phone in 1997. He was visiting from Argentina and had brought his British girlfriend Jenny with him to meet the family. "I need your advice. Can I come in to talk with you?"

"Of course. When do you want to come in?" I asked. I was in my office at Budget Real Estate on Santa Monica Boulevard in West Los Angeles. Budget owned and operated the roughly fifty properties I owned in Southern California. I was in the midst of trying to get a roofing contractor to go back to fix a leak in a roof he had replaced just two months prior. He was pushing back, saying that the leak must be coming from a leaky pipe, which I was confident was not the case. I was so distracted by the issue that I was only half paying attention to what Charles was saying.

"Can I come now?" he asked.

"Yeah, sure," I said, a bit surprised by the urgency. The timing certainly wasn't perfect, but this was my brother.

When Charles walked into my office, he looked somber and serious. "Hi, Jorge," he said.

"Hey, Charles. Have a seat," I said, motioning to the chair across my desk.

"Thanks," he said as he sat down. He immediately slumped into the chair.

"How do you like being back in SoCal?" I asked.

"It's going well. I've seen some old friends," he said. "But I am stressed." He sounded distraught.

"What's going on?" I asked.

"Here's my problem: before I moved to Argentina, I had a student loan of sixteen thousand dollars from when I went to UCLA plus twenty-six thousand dollars on credit cards," he said. I noticed he was sweating, even though the temperature was moderate.

"Okay," I said.

"My job writing for the *Buenos Aires Herald* doesn't pay that much," he said. "I can only make the minimum payments. My balances are hardly going down."

"The minimum payments are mostly interest," I said. "They don't do much to chip away your principal balance."

"I did the calculations," he said, sounding dejected.

"After paying my living expenses, I can pay everything else to my creditors. Even if I factor in some raises, paying everything off will take thirteen years."

"I see," I said, unsure where he was going with this.

"The problem is Jenny," he said. He wiped some sweat, which had built up on his forehead.

"She seems nice," I said, now puzzled. Jenny worked as a web developer, got along well with the family, and had good musical taste. "She likes The Cranberries," I commented. Jenny also shared the same name and home country as our mom.

"The problem is that I want to marry Jenny," he said, "and start a family. But I cannot see how I can afford to do this and also pay my debts."

"You want to stay in Argentina?" I asked.

"Yes, for now," he said. "Eventually, we'll probably move back here."

This conversation happened almost a decade prior to my Woodland Meadows meltdown. I had yet to learn the Debt Cleanse tactics that I share today. Nevertheless, I pondered his situation for a minute. I noticed Charles shift in his seat a few times.

"Charles, you're living in Argentina. All the debt is in the US, and none of the debts are overly large," I finally said. "Don't pay."

"None of them?" he asked.

"None of them," I said.

"What will the creditors do?" he asked.

"Probably call and write letters," I said. "But you will be in Argentina, so there is nothing they can really do."

"I do freelance writing work for some American companies," he said, still sounding worried. "Could they intercept what I earn?"

"Probably not," I said. "They'd have to go to court. The debts are probably too small for them to really bother."

"What about the student loan?" he said. "It's government backed. Can I get in trouble?"

"Same story," I said. "Even at sixteen thousand dollars, that's too small to chase you hard."

"Can they extradite me?" he asked

"No," I said. "Extradition is usually only for criminal matters."

"So what's the downside?" he asked, sounding a bit more upbeat. He sat up a little straighter in his chair.

"Your credit will be messed up," I said. "Outside of that, you should be fine."

"What if I want to buy a house later," he said. "In the US."

"After seven years, the unpaid debts should drop from your credit report," I said.

"That all makes sense," he said, suddenly beaming. "What a relief." He got up to leave. As he turned, I noticed that the back of his shirt was soaked with sweat. "Thanks for the advice, Jorge."

"No problem," I said.

Seventeen years later, I shared Charles' story with my wife as we made our way to Jerry's Famous Deli in Studio City, California. We were meeting Emily and her friend Amber for breakfast as part of a weekend trip to Southern California. I was out to visit my parents and siblings. Amber was in a debt bind and needed some advice.

Are all Emily's friends broke? I remembered thinking when Emily scheduled the meeting, before realizing that most Americans are insolvent, or close to it. The date was October 25, 2014.

"Charles was your first Debt Cleanse," Verria said.

"I never thought about it like that," I said. "I was just happy to help him."

"There's Jerry's," Verria said, as I pulled into the left lane to turn.

"At the time, I remember wondering how many graduates faced similar choices," I said. "Maybe they did not realize that not paying their debts was an option."

"Most people just assume you have to pay your debts," Verria said, "especially student loans."

"Our youth shouldn't have to decide between paying their debts and chasing their dreams, like getting married and starting a family," I said. "Or traveling, or starting a business, or any other pursuit."

I opened the door for Verria as we entered Jerry's.

"Table for four," I advised the hostess.

"Do you see Emily?" Verria asked.

"No. She's usually late," I said. I flicked my AHP business card into a jar with a handwritten sign: "Free Lunch Drawing."

"Right this way," the hostess said. She had a button on which read, "Life begins at the end of your comfort zone." We followed her to a booth in the back of the restaurant.

"There's Emily," I said as we sat down. Emily was near the front looking around. She looked well. You would never have known that she went through an unaffordable debt crisis. I guessed I didn't have any telling marks from my debt battles either. You needed to look into our psyches to see the scars.

I started walking over. "Hey, Emily!"

"Hi, Mr. Newbery!" Emily exclaimed with a grin. She came over and gave me a hug and kiss—a standard Emily greeting.

"Come on back," I said. We started walking to the table.

"Hi, Verria," Emily said.

"Oh hi, Emily," said Verria, getting up. They exchanged a hug and kiss. I had introduced them a few years back, and we had shared five or six meals. We all sat down.

"Amber is running late," Emily said. "She should be here in fifteen minutes."

"I'm impressed, Emily," I said.

"Why?" Emily asked.

"You're only five minutes late," I said. "That's good for you."

"I know," Emily said, as she blushed. We all laughed. "I'm trying to get better at that. I set my car clock and all the clocks in my home ten minutes fast."

"Glad to hear your self-deception is working out," I said. "So what's up Emily?"

"Got a new job as a loan agent," Emily said. "Plus I still do the dog grooming part time."

"I've always been impressed by your resiliency, Emily," said Verria. "You never let yourself get down, even when everything is going against you. You're like Jorge in that respect."

"I've had some tough times," said Emily. "But I just make the best of everything."

"That's how you make it in life," I said. "Make the best of imperfect situations."

"Preach," said Emily.

"Seriously, though, when bad stuff happens," I said. "I'm always thinking, 'Dang, why do I get dealt the bad hands when everyone else has easy hands?' But then I catch myself and realize that everyone gets dealt bad hands at some point. Everyone can do well with the easy hands. The difference between success and failure is how you play the bad hands."

"That's my honey," said Verria. "Always finding the ace even in the worst of times."

"Bring on the bad hands," I said. "I'll play them. And I can show others how to play them, too."

"Speaking of which, there's Amber," said Emily. "Amber, over here!"

"I don't think she heard you," I said, getting up. "I'll go and get her."

"Thanks," said Emily.

"Hi," I said. "Are you Amber?"

"Yes," she said. Amber was white, maybe fifty, and petite with blond hair, blue eyes, and an athletic build. She was wearing Lululemon yoga pants, but not the see-through kind.

"I'm Jorge," I said. We shook hands and started walking back.

Greetings and introductions were made at the table before we settled in to get down to the purpose of the meeting.

"What's going on, Amber?" I asked, as she unfolded her napkin.

"Emily told me that I could ask you about debt," Amber said.

"They call me Debt Threat," I said, recalling my conversation with Juju at the Chicago conference. Everyone started laughing.

"Who calls you Debt Threat?" asked Verria.

"Someone I met in Chicago," I said. "Sounds cool, right? I'm going to start using it."

"Using it *when*?" asked Verria, sounding skeptical.

"I don't know, just around," I said. "When we go to

galas, they can announce our entrance."

"We don't go to galas," Verria said.

"But, if we did, they would announce our arrival," I said. "Please welcome Debt Threat and the Debt Brunette." We all laughed.

"So Amber," I said. "Debt Threat is at your service."

"Okay, here's the story. My husband and I were laid off in 2009. We both had manufacturing jobs in Torrance," Amber said. "We started thinking of alternative careers as we figured that the manufacturing jobs were not coming back."

"Unless you moved to China," added Emily.

"Our eldest child had graduated and was going to college," Amber said. "We started seeing these ads on the Internet: 'Obama wants you to go back to school.'"

"I've seen those," I said.

"We thought we could all go to college together," Amber said. "The three of us."

"Sounds like a good opportunity," Verria said. "Family bonding."

"That's what we thought, but we were naive," Amber said. "We bought into all the 'Change You Can Believe In' stuff. We got taken."

"Taken?" I said.

"Yes, taken. And now we need help," Amber said. "Debt Threat help."

"Okay," I said, nudging Verria. The nickname was catching on.

"To go back to school, we were all offered student loans," Amber said. "Loans for tuition, books, housing costs, everything. All we had to do was sign on the dotted line."

"They make getting the loans too easy," Emily said. "No real qualifying. The lenders seem to think that everyone will graduate with a high-paying job."

"That's right. We thought that our new skills could be parlayed into rewarding careers," said Amber. "We believed that we could easily afford to pay them back."

"There should be some better disclosures," I said, "warning students that they are unlikely to get jobs that will actually allow them to promptly payoff their loans."

"Yes," said Emily, "because otherwise people end up with lifetimes of debt."

"Debt slaves," I said.

"We need to all become debt *threats*," said Emily. "Not debt slaves."

"Exactly," I said. "Spread the word that people don't have to repay their unaffordable debts, including student loans."

"But that's why I wanted to talk to you, Debt Threat," said Amber. "Because I hear that student debt has special powers and people can't get rid of it."

"That's only partially true," I said. "Student loans are one of the few debts that cannot generally be discharged by bankruptcy, whether private or federal-government backed. To get a discharge, a debtor will need to assert undue hardship: poverty, little likelihood of improved circumstances, and that a good faith effort has been made to pay."

"Yes," said Amber. "That's what I was afraid of. We're doing badly, but we are all working."

"Wait, there's hope," I said. "Hope you can believe in."

"That's what Obama said in 2008," said Emily.

"Yes, but this time it's true," I said. "Student loans come in two flavors: private and government backed."

"We have both," said Amber.

"For the private loans," I said, "your creditor needs to sue you to obtain a judgment and garnish or levy. The strategy is just like a credit card or any other unsecured creditor."

"Okay," Amber said.

"Stop paying, ignore the creditors, dispute the debts, and identify and exploit deficiencies," I said. "The standard Debt Cleanse playbook."

"I've told Amber about all that," said Emily. "She just didn't think it would work for student loans."

"Government-backed loans are more challenging," I said, as I played with my fork.

"I knew it," said Amber, sounding resigned.

"First, there is no statute of limitations to collect," I said. "Also, judgments are not needed in order to garnish wages, levy bank accounts, or even divert income tax refunds and portions of Social Security or other benefits."

"Ugh, we're trapped," said Amber. I heard heavy frustration in her voice.

"Not trapped," I said. "Before taking these actions, the Department of Education or a guaranty agency is required to send a thirty-day notice to your last known address."

"What can we do with the notice?" asked Amber, perking up.

"This notice provides you rights to inspect and copy your records related to the debt," I said, "and to request a hearing concerning the existence, amount, or current enforceability of the debt."

"That sounds like going to court against a creditor," said Emily.

"Exactly," I said. "You'll need to request records within twenty days of the date of the notice, and a hearing within thirty days."

"Okay," Amber said.

"The only exception is for FFEL loans," I said. "Then the requests need to be made within fifteen days."

"What's FFEL?" asked Emily.

"Federal Family Education Loan," I said. "FFEL was a public-private partnership, with taxpayer dollars subsidizing private lenders making government-backed loans."

"Sounds like another handout to the creditors," said Emily.

"Yes, the program was eliminated in 2010," I said. "The

government estimated FFELs were wasting eight billion dollars of taxpayer dollars a year."

"Taking eight billion dollars a year from the people and giving the money to the elite creditors?" said Emily. "I would figure they would expand a program like that." We all laughed, and Emily and Amber exchanged a high five.

We took a break from the conversation to put in our orders with our waitress.

"Poached eggs," Verria said, "how adventurous of you."

"What can I say? I'm a risk taker," I smiled back at her.

"Okay, so the government loans?" asked Amber, intent on getting the conversation back to the topic at hand.

"When you get the notices," I said. "Demand the documents and records. Request an oral in-person hearing. Going in person will be more of a burden for you, but also for the Board of Education. Do not ask for an oral telephone hearing or a paper hearing. Imagine exchanging or submitting documents via phone versus in person—it just isn't as effective. Also, getting in front of other human beings face-to-face is much more likely to result in a positive outcome, or at least make some progress."

"What form do I use to make these requests?" Amber asked, listening intently.

"They're on my site, debtcleanse.com," I said. "I'll e-mail you a link."

"I'll text you her e-mail address," said Emily.

"When you send in the request," I said, "attach a copy

of the government's notice and send by certified mail, return receipt requested."

"Got that," Amber said.

"Oral hearings are usually heard in Washington, DC, Atlanta, Chicago, and San Francisco," I said.

"Road trip!" said Emily.

"You and/or your attorney will need to travel at your expense," I said. "This may seem like a burdensome expenditure, but use the money from your settlement wallet. Your investment is likely to be worthwhile. Do you know what the settlement wallet is?"

"Yes, Emily told me that is where I save the money when I stop paying my unaffordable debts," Amber said.

"You can then use these monies to settle your debts at big discounts and pay legal fees," I said. "You can even take a trip to San Francisco to attend the government student loan hearing. But don't use the money to go on a family vacation." I looked directly at Emily.

"What?" Emily asked with a feigned look of surprise.

"So instead of making payments on your student loans, you are using that same money to pay for an attorney and travel costs," I said. "Student loans are typically large enough that engaging an attorney is wise, particularly one with student loan debt defense experience. We are going to put together a directory on debtcleanse.com. In the meantime, you can find one by Googling student loan defense attorneys and checking their Yelp reviews."

"Okay," Amber said. "I am going to go home and sort through all the notices I have received. What if the deadline to request a hearing and the documents has already passed?"

"That's fine. Even if the time deadlines have passed, or even if the government was already garnishing your wages or taking other actions, you could still request documents and a hearing," I said. "However, the garnishment or other action will typically continue until the matter is resolved."

"But if I request before the deadline, then they cannot garnish or levy, right?" asked Amber.

"That's right," I said. "Everything is on hold until they prove that you owe the money, that the amount they claim is due, that they own the loan, and that they have the books and records to prove all this."

"But these are the government and big banks," Amber said. "Surely, their records are straight."

Emily and I started laughing.

"That's not the case," Emily said. "The big banks are the worst."

"The government is no better," I said. "Deficiencies, errors, missing documents,"

"So I could win?" said Amber. She sounded hopeful.

"You might," I said. "But the more likely outcome is that you lose. However, you can then sue the guaranty agency, US Department of Education, debt holder, servicer, and school. Exploit deficiencies and push to settle the student loans for pennies on the dollar."

"Settling these would be a win for me," said Amber. "And my family."

"So where are you working now?" asked Verria.

"At Target, as a cashier," Amber said. "For eight dollars and sixty-seven cents an hour. My husband and daughter work there, too."

"That sounds convenient," said Verria.

"It is, but the paychecks aren't convenient," said Amber. "Don't get me wrong. Target is fine to work for, and we are happy to have steady work."

"I shop at Target all the time," said Emily. "Can you get me a discount?"

"It's a fifteen percent discount," Amber said. "But just for immediate family."

"Oh," said Emily.

"The problem is that we are three college graduates with almost two hundred thousand dollars in student loans between us. My daughter Lisa graduated in marketing. I got an interior design degree, and my husband got one in computer engineering," said Amber. "And the only work we can find is at Target."

"You didn't need to go to college to work at Target," Verria said.

"Exactly," Amber said. "The whole family would have been better off if we hadn't gone to college."

"That's sad," said Verria.

"We have two more in high school. We've told them that they can go to college if they want," Amber said. "But they must promise not to take out any student loans. They can go to a community college and work part time, or skip college and go straight to work. They can travel, see the world, join a rock band, or even affiliate with a commune. Really. They can do whatever they want as long as they do not take out any student loans."

"Amen," said Emily. "No more debt."

"You know, years ago I was anxious about what could happen when my oldest would go to college," Amber said. "Would we lose touch, would she use drugs or alcohol, or get pregnant? But you know what?"

"What?" Emily asked.

"My worries were all misplaced," said Amber. "My worry should have been that she took out student loans. They do more damage than losing touch, drugs, alcohol, or even getting pregnant."

We all sat silently for a few minutes.

"Lisa wanted to get a job in marketing," Amber said. "She was so full of dreams for her future."

"I remember for her sixteenth birthday, Lisa sent out fortune cookies inscribed with 'You're Invited'," said Emily. "The invitation was folded up inside the cookie. That was so cute and original."

"I remember that. She always was coming up with genius marketing ideas," said Amber. "She got good grades in high school and college."

"She's a smart girl," said Emily.

"But no one wanted to hire her for a marketing job," Amber said. "She went on dozens of interviews. She posted all the rejection letters on her bedroom wall. Each letter seemed to drain another ounce of her optimism."

"So sad," said Emily.

"My husband and I can take working at Target. We can't pay our bills, but we have an okay life, you know?" said Amber. "We have three healthy kids."

"They're good kids," said Emily.

"I feel the worst for Lisa. I watch her restocking shelves in her Target uniform, and I know her dreams have evaporated," Amber said. "Now her hope is to marry a man with some money or a good job. She thinks that as soon as she gets married and has kids, she will have some security. Her future should not depend on a man."

Silence enveloped our table again. However, joy was about to return, at least for most of us.

"Here's the food," I said eagerly, eyeing our server as she made her way to the back.

"Finally," said Verria.

"Veggie omelet?" the server asked.

"Here," said Verria. Everyone's plates were delivered, except for mine.

"Your breakfast will be a few more minutes," the server said. "The eggs are still poaching." My eyes met Verria's.

"I just got dealt a bad hand," I said, still looking at Verria. "Can I have some of yours?" She pulled the plate closer to her, away from me. I looked at Emily and Amber, and they both pulled their plates back as well.

"Well," I said. "You all may as well all start eating. I'll sit over here famished, wasting away."

"Debt Threat dies of starvation at Jerry's Deli," Amber said. "I can see the headlines now."

"I guess Americans will have to figure out their debt problems on their own," I said.

"Two bites, that's all," Verria said, relenting and pushing her plate toward me. I reached over with my fork and tried to get the largest forkful I could. Her omelet looked scrumptious, although that may have been partially attributed to my extreme hunger.

"Hey, that counts as two bites," said Verria, sounding miffed.

"You said *two*," I said slowly, my mouth almost full. "That was only one." I reached my fork over again. "You can have some of my eggs," I said.

Then I returned my attention to the other side of the table.

"Amber," I said. "Sallie Mae has faced class action lawsuits almost every year since being privatized in 1997."

"What is Sallie Mae?" asked Emily.

"Sallie Mae used to be a government-sponsored enterprise similar to Fannie Mae and Freddie Mac," I said.

"Now Sallie Mae is a for-profit publicly traded company and the largest private profiteer of student debt. They own nearly twenty percent of the over one trillion dollars in outstanding student loan debt in the US."

"Sounds like a big bully," said Emily.

"There have been some favorable class action outcomes for borrowers," I said. "In 2012, there was a twenty-four-million-dollar settlement, a seventy-six-million-dollar settlement in 2013, and a one-hundred-million-dollar settlement in 2014."

"Big money!" said Emily. "Amber is in the money!"

"Not exactly," I said. "Big chunks of these lawsuits often end up going to the attorneys who bring the actions, while those who were actually damaged typically receive token sums."

"Dang," said Emily.

"Still, Amber and her family may be able to benefit from these actions," I said. "They can either join the class, or use the class action's allegations as part of their defense and offense against Sallie Mae or one of their guaranty agencies."

"That's helpful. Thanks," said Amber. "You know, I still don't understand what is happening to this country."

"How so?" I asked.

"My daughter went to UCLA," Amber said. "When my brother went there in 1980, the tuition was $776. My daughter's tuition was $13,218. That's a seventeen-hundred-percent increase. I remember thinking that something's not right here."

"Something does seem wrong," said Emily.

"So I checked the rate of inflation over that time period," Amber said. "It was one hundred and seventy-three percent. So I kept asking myself what I was missing. One-hundred-and-seventy-three percent inflation rate, but UCLA tuition went up seventeen hundred percent. It wasn't just UCLA: the average tuition nationwide went up over five hundred percent in the same time period."

"That doesn't make sense," said Emily.

"Part of the reason is that government spending on higher education in 2011 dropped over forty percent since 1980," said Amber.

"But do you know why that happened?" I asked.

"No," Amber said.

"Sallie Mae employs sixty-three lobbyists armed with millions to donate to politicians," I said. "These lobbyists encourage states to reduce and eliminate taxpayer support for higher education, which drives up the demand for Sallie Mae's predatory loans."

"That's terrible," said Amber.

"It's wrong," said Emily.

Hopeful high school and college students with big dreams are enticed to enslave themselves to lifetimes of student debt. Typically, students' dreams are unfulfilled. However, in earning over $225 million in the student loan business between 1999 and 2004, Sallie Mae CEO Albert Lord got to fulfill *his* dream: he built a private eighteen-hole golf course on 335 acres.

"There's another reason as well," I said. "In the last decade, colleges have become more Wall Street than Main Street. In 1980, college presidents typically came from lives in academia—a noble but typically not super financially rewarding pursuit."

"My dad was a teacher," said Amber. "He loved his work, but his pay wasn't great."

"Today, many college presidents come from business and politics," I said. "They typically sell themselves as being able to bring efficiency to running colleges like a business."

"They don't seem too efficient to me," Amber said. "At least not for the students."

"College presidents receive generous compensation packages, sometimes in the millions of dollars," I said. "Next, they create administrative positions and fill them with friends or those whose loyalty they buy with fat salaries."

"That's terrible," said Emily.

"Forty years ago, there were close to twice as many faculty as administrators and staffers," I said. "By 2005, there were more administrators and staffers than full-time faculty. Further, the full-time faculty is often made up of numerous part-time professors."

"What do all these administrators and staffers do?" asked Amber.

"Well, they aren't teaching," I said.

"Isn't that the primary mission of colleges?" asked Amber. "To teach?"

"That's secondary," I said. "First, they need to generate revenue, which they do by maximizing income. They peddle loans to students who otherwise could not afford to pay the exorbitant costs of education. Second, they need to minimize expenses, which they do by minimizing the wages and benefits paid to faculty."

"Sounds like Wall Street," said Amber.

"Exactly," I said. "That's why students get saddled with lifetimes of debt and you hear stories of faculty sleeping in homeless shelters, going without health insurance, living on food stamps, and unable to live normal lives."

"My family is about two steps from all that," Amber said. "We already get food stamps."

"Worse, the college presidents leading this march to the death of our nation's higher education system are getting paid handsomely," I said. "In 2013, Ohio State University president E. Gordon Gee earned over six million dollars."

"Six million dollars!" Amber said. "What did he do for that?"

"I'm not against people earning money," I said. "If President Gee had somehow found a way to teach students effectively and affordably, then this compensation might have been deserved. This country is driven by innovation. Visionaries who take risks and improve society should be rewarded for their ingenuity."

"What did President Gee do to teach students efficiently and affordably?" asked Emily.

"That's just it. He did nothing," I said. "Under his tenure, debt among OSU students grew twenty-three percent faster than the national average. In fact, the student debt crisis is worse at state schools with the highest-paid presidents."

"Fuckers!" blurted Amber, her face red with rage.

We all looked at her.

"I'm sorry," Amber said, composing herself. "Hearing this makes me mad."

"Here you go," said the server proudly as she plopped down my plate. My breakfast didn't look nearly as good as the others.

I took a mouthful. The eggs were over-poached and dry. I motioned to Verria as if to say, "Want some?" She plunked a fork into the center of one of the poached eggs, but it barely pierced the egg.

"Wow, those eggs are well-done," said Verria.

"Yours is better," I said, eyeing her half-finished veggie omelet. "Want to trade?"

"Nope, but I'm confused about something," Verria said. "Ohio State is a state school. UCLA is a state school. Who is supposed to be in charge over all this?"

"Take a deep breath, Amber," I said. "This might be infuriating."

"Oh no," Amber said. I heard her inhale, followed by a long exhale. It sounded like a yoga class.

"At Ohio State," I said. "There is a board of trustees, which includes Abigail Wexner, wife of Les Wexner, who has a net worth of $5.8 billion earned from businesses such as Victoria's Secret; Timothy P. Smucker, who earns almost $5 million annually as CEO of J.M. Smucker; and Ronald Ratner, who earned over $1.2 million in 2013."

"Those are some really rich people," said Amber, sounding upset.

"Exactly," I said. "Control of these public institutions of higher education has been taken over by the financial elite. These types often hand around administrative jobs and bonuses as political favors."

"Is this just at Ohio State?" Emily asked.

"No," I said. "This is a nationwide epidemic."

"How depressing," Amber said, still fuming with ire.

"The University of California is governed by a board of regents who are essentially appointed to ensure that the UC runs efficiently as a business," I said. "Regents include multi-millionaires such as Richard Blum, husband of US Senator Dianne Feinstein, who proclaims his background in education is an asset."

"Well at least he has one. That's good," said Emily.

"Not in this case," I said. "Blum's privately owned investment firm, Blum Capital Partners, owns for-profit colleges whose primary sources of revenue are federally guaranteed student loans and grants authorized by Congress."

"That sounds like a conflict of interest," said Amber, her voice boiling. "His wife is a senator and he could benefit from her votes."

"Welcome to America," I said. "It gets even worse. Blum's for-profit college company is Career Education Corporation, which, in 2010, reported that over eighty-five percent of total revenue consisted of federal education funds. Over ninety-six percent of CEC students obtained student loans."

"My husband went to CEC," said Amber. "They told him they had a ninety-nine percent job placement rate for computer engineering graduates. They totally misled us."

"CEC spent about fifteen hundred dollars per student on instruction in 2009, compared to over three thousand dollars per student on marketing, and earned fifteen hundred dollars per student in profit," I said.

"They spent twice as much on marketing as instruction?" asked Emily. "Fuckers."

"Most graduates end up in jobs no better than they could have obtained without CEC's education," I said. "But now the students get stuck repaying these huge loans to pay for worthless educations. And most didn't even graduate."

"This is so messed up. My family and I got sold on our

big dreams," said Amber. "We tried to do the right thing, but instead we ended up enslaved to lifetimes of student loan debt."

"I'm sorry that it worked out that way," I said.

"What did you say earlier?" Amber asked.

"About what?" I asked.

"About bad hands," Amber said.

"If you are dealt a bad hand, just make the best of it," I said. "Kind of like me and these eggs."

"That's what we're going to do," Amber said. "We'll do the hearings, request the documents, sue 'em all, and make the best of this mess."

"Good attitude," I said.

"Listen, I got to get to Target," Amber said. "I really appreciate all your insight. I feel better now, like I have a plan." She pulled her wallet out of her purse to pay for her meal.

"No, Amber, we got this," I said, standing up. "I am sorry to hear your story, but I wish you and your family well. Let me know if you have any questions." I reached out my hand to shake Amber's. Instead, she got up and walked out of the booth toward me. Then she gave me a big hug. The hug lasted a bit too long and, as I glanced at Verria, I caught a glare.

"I've got to go, too," said Emily. "Dog grooming today." Emily walked over and gave me a hug and a kiss. Emily's seemed to be of normal duration, but Verria's glare appeared to harden further.

"Bye to both of you," Verria and I both said as Emily and Amber walked away. I finished eating.

The weight of student loans robs graduates of the dreams they probably went to college for in the first place. The payments of these exorbitant loans, coupled with the extreme competition within a market flooded with degree-carrying applicants, make it difficult (if not impossible) to put together the life each of us has envisioned—the life each of us deserves. Long before I knew what I know now, the day Charles asked me for advice, I still knew that my brother deserved the future he wanted far more than the banks deserved the thousands of dollars in interest they planned to charge him for the next thirteen years. Thankfully, he agreed.

The day after my brother left my office, he proposed to Jenny. She said yes, and they have been married fifteen years and have three healthy children. He was ready to postpone marriage and raising a family for a more than a decade to allow him time to pay off his debt. However, he chose himself and his family over his creditors and never made another payment on any of the debt he left behind in the United States, including his student loan. When I see him now, he's happy and no longer sweats excessively. The debts all died, and Charles has gone on to a successful journalism career. He achieved the future he deserved, just as I hope we all can.

CHAPTER 7

I AM CONTAMINATED

NOVEMBER 6, 2014. I DECIDED I NEEDED A BREAK. For five months, I had juggled growing American Homeowner Preservation with writing and speaking engagements. As AHP acquired more unaffordable debt at big discounts, I helped recruit and train new AHP staff, pitch AHP to new investors and debt sellers, and traveled to speak at conferences across the country to spread the word. To stay fit and sane, I squeezed in solo runs whenever I could. However, I was tired and needed the camaraderie of some familiar faces. Fortunately, I was back home in Chicago.

At 6:00 p.m., I changed into my running gear at AHP and started running north on Michigan Avenue to Niketown, the fitness brand's upscale flagship store, to join the Thursday night training run organized there, which was typically seven miles on the lakefront. There are often some speedy runners there and while I typically loved to run at the front of the pack with them, I was out of race-ready condition. I arrived just as the run started and was immediately greeted by a running buddy.

"Hi, Jorge!" said Alice, as we headed out. She was maybe five feet seven, brunette, and in her mid-twenties; she looked like a younger version of Danica Patrick, the race car driver. Alice was fit, toned, and fast. We often ended up running together at the front. I knew the easygoing run I had pictured for myself had gone out the window. "Welcome back."

"Hi, Alice," I said. "Small-size group tonight." There were maybe a dozen of us. The group swelled to over fifty at times.

"Yes, a lot of people are still taking it easy after Chicago," Alice said, referring to the Chicago Marathon three weeks prior. "We've missed you. Where have you been?"

"I've been busy with work and writing a book," I said, a bit haltingly, as I endured what felt like a seven-minute-per-mile pace. Just a couple of years ago, I could run this pace for a marathon or longer. But priorities shift and, that evening, I could feel myself straining.

"Really, what kind of book?" she asked.

We were running east toward the lakefront path. Most of the group fell behind, leaving Alice, another runner named Chris, and I alone out front. Chris was about the same age as Alice, taller than me, probably six feet four inches, and lanky. With his sandy blond hair, he looked more like a surfer than a Midwestern runner.

"I show people how to manage debt," I said, trying to be diplomatic and not hoping for a long conversation. The pace made talking a challenge.

"My parents should talk to you," she said.

"Why is that?" I asked. I was looking for a break from thinking about debt, but everywhere I go there are Americans mired in unaffordable debt.

"They've had some troubles," she said.

Don't ask what kind, I thought.

"What kind of troubles?" asked Chris.

"My dad opened a Quiznos with his best friend about four years ago," she said. "They both put all their savings in, plus took out a Small Business Administration loan. They were really excited."

"I like Quiznos sandwiches," Chris said. "But they always seem overpriced to me."

"Subway is better," I said. "Healthier and cheaper."

"The prices are set by the company," Alice said. "But the bigger problem was that Quiznos forced the franchisees to buy all their supplies and ingredients from one company."

"Maybe they got bulk discounts?" I proffered. We got stopped by a red light, which allowed me a minute to catch my breath. I looked at Alice, who looked peppy and comfortable. She was running in place at the stoplight. I was just standing, as was Chris. Although I was keeping up, I could hear from our breathing that I was exerting more than both of them.

"You would think that," Alice said. "But the opposite was true. The supplier was overcharging for everything."

"That doesn't make sense," I said. We started running again.

"It turns out that the supplier was a Quiznos affiliate and generated a lot of revenue for the company," said Alice, sounding agitated. "But the franchisees could not make a profit with the company-mandated pricing and the high costs of supplies."

Franchise disclosure documents reveal that Quiznos has collected much more money from their affiliate, American Food Distributors LLC, selling overpriced food and supplies to franchisees than it took in from royalties based on sandwich sales.

"So what happened with your dad and his friend?" I asked.

"They both quit their regular jobs to run the store," she said. "They were planning to open several more Quiznos stores with all the money they expected to make."

"Big plans," I said.

"But the sales were never quite enough," she lamented. "They were breaking even, but neither of them was getting paid, even though they worked full time."

"For how long?" I asked.

"Several years. It seemed like forever," she said. "They kept thinking that things were about to turn around, but they never did. Dad started using credit cards to pay living expenses. My mom works, but she barely makes enough to pay the mortgage."

"Sounds terrible," Chris said.

"It was," she said. "I was going to school. But I quit and started working at the shop. At first they paid me, but eventually I just worked for free. I was trying to do my share to help my dad. He supported me all those years growing up."

"That's nice of you," I said.

"At some point, though, I started to think the whole situation was stupid," she said. "My dad, his friend, and I were all working for free just to try to keep everything going. We were just slaving away to pay the inflated costs of the supplier so Quiznos corporate could get rich."

"What a bad situation," I said. "Quiznos corporate was siphoning off whatever they could get off your family."

The chain is owned by Wall Street hedge fund Avenue Capital Group. In 2006, Quiznos underwent a leveraged buyout, which saddled the company with $950 million in debt. By 2012, when the company was struggling with an unaffordable debt load, Avenue took over. In 2014, unable to turn fortunes around, Quiznos filed for bankruptcy.

"I tried to talk to my dad," she said. "But he would get angry. Not at me, but just the situation. All my years growing up, I rarely saw him mad. With that Quiznos, he was upset all the time. I think he felt hopeless. Then he started drinking. Everything was going badly."

"I'm not going to eat at Quiznos anymore," said Chris.

"This is tragic," I said.

"It gets worse," said Alice. I had the feeling that maybe she hadn't confessed all of this to anyone else before. I felt a tinge special that she was so willing to share so much with Chris and me as we ran north along the lakefront. Telling the stories contaminating your head may be the best therapy. Drain the decay from your brain and make room for new thought to replace the rot. It seemed as though Alice was doing exactly that as we ran.

"What happened?" I asked.

"My dad never had any problems with alcohol before. I mean, he drank, but never too much," she said. "But now he started drinking all the time, and it started to seem like he was losing control of it. I think he drank to escape all the debts his venture had wrecked on the family. It's crazy, but when this started, all he was trying to do was provide a better life for us."

"This is so sad," said Chris.

"When my dad started slipping, my mom started coming from her regular job directly to the Quiznos every night and on the weekends to help out," she said. "This fucking Quiznos was destroying our family."

I gazed out at Lake Michigan. The strong waves were

lapping over the shore walls like teams of water molecules trying to escape the lake. I blinked and saw a sea of American debtors, all wanting to flee the confines of the lake. Maybe if they splashed hard enough, they could crest the walls and find a better life free of debt. However, one molecule by itself could not survive. There needed to be a mass breakout so they could pool together and create a better lake for everyone.

We ran in silence for a few minutes. The headwind had grown stiff, and I tucked in behind Chris to get a bit of shelter. Chris got behind Alice, but the height difference resulted in minimal cover.

"What happened in the end?" asked Chris. "With your family's Quiznos?" We had turned around to head back, so the wind was now at our backs.

"My mom made my dad go to AA meetings while we tried to run the store," she said. "But he didn't do that well. He kept missing meetings; sometimes he wouldn't come home at night. We didn't know what to do."

"He needed to want the change," I said. "Some people aren't ready to change until something really bad happens."

"It did," she said. "He got in a car accident that hospitalized two DePaul students. My dad was okay, thankfully, but he was arrested for DUI."

"Were the students okay?" asked Chris.

"They both ended up fully recovered," she said. "But that was the wake-up call. We closed the Quiznos. Now, my dad is going to the meetings."

"Glad it ended," said Chris.

"But that's the thing. It did *not* end," she said. "Now the landlord has sued my parents and his best friend because they personally guaranteed the lease. Plus, they fell behind on all of the credit cards and the SBA loan. They'll probably sue next. Finally, my dad could go to prison for the DUI."

"I'm only going to Subway from now on," said Chris.

"I can help. Not with the DUI, but with everything else," I said. "Here's what your parents should do."

We turned to take the walkway under Lake Shore Drive just north of Navy Pier. We were getting near the end and my forty-nine-year old legs had kept up with those young'uns. Luckily, all the talking kept the pace reasonable.

"Watch the rut," said Chris, as we navigated a broken sidewalk, representing a rather large trip hazard.

"First, they need to stop paying everything," I said.

"The only thing they are paying right now is the mortgage," she said. "You want them to stop paying the mortgage?"

"Can they afford to pay the mortgage?" I asked.

"Not really," she said. "They are borrowing from family to keep it up. The legal fees for the DUI are a drain." We cruised to a stop in front of Niketown.

"Tell them to stop paying everything," I said, turning back to face Alice. "And stop borrowing from family. Or have them call me, and I will tell them." We walked into Niketown to stay warm.

"I'm not sure I understand," she said, sounding bewildered. "I thought your book was about *managing* debt?"

"Yes, I show people how to manage unaffordable debt by not paying," I said. "Borrowers can gain leverage by not paying, exploiting deficiencies, and eventually settling debts at big discounts, or not paying at all."

"Is that legal?" asked Chris.

"Yes, many times we use the legal system as part of the settlement process," I said. "It's legal."

"To say that to stop paying is the cure to unaffordable debt..." she said, her voice trailing. "I'm unsure how that's going to improve the situation. It sounds like it will make it worse."

"But you said your parents are already not paying everything except the mortgage," I said.

"That's because they can't afford to pay," she said. "They would pay if they could."

"But if they can't afford to pay, wouldn't it be better to proactively stop paying?" I asked. "Rather than borrowing from friends and family to go deeper in debt to pay obligations they can't afford anyway? Where is this going to end?"

I looked at Alice. She appeared upset, like a wave of reality had just crashed onto her. I had seen that reaction happen in so many just like her. The weight of unaffordable debt and the nonstop treadmill of payments and fees was heavy and impossible to avoid forever. Her eyes looked moist, like she was about to cry.

"I'm sorry," I said. "I didn't mean to trouble you."

Our eyes met. She had soft cheeks and wise eyes. She was a pretty girl. Too young to be so caught up in her parents' challenges. She had a lifetime of her own challenges ahead. We all do.

Say something, I thought. Her silence was making me uncomfortable.

"Do you want to go to dinner?" she finally asked. I was unsure where that came from. I clasped my hands in front of me, making sure that my wedding band was plainly visible. She chuckled and grinned. "Dinner *with my parents*. They are coming to pick me up now."

"I don't have a change of clothes," I said.

"Neither do I," she said. "We're just going for sandwiches."

"Quiznos?" I asked. We both started laughing.

"Subway, probably," she said. "You want to come, Chris?"

"No," said Chris. "I've got to get home."

Ten minutes later, an older Honda Accord pulled up. "Mom and Dad," Alice said. "This is Jorge. He is coming to dinner with us."

I reached out my hand.

"I'm Steve," said Alice's father as we shook hands.

"I'm Martha," said Alice's mother as we exchanged smiles. Alice and I settled in the car. Martha was driving. I suspected that Steve's driver's license might have been suspended.

"Does Subway sound good to both of you?" asked Steve.

"Sure," we said. Alice and I smiled at each other, and she let out a giggle.

We walked into the Subway on State Street near Ontario Street. Martha appeared to be in her early fifties and looked very much like an older Alice. Like her daughter, Martha looked fit. She was dressed in a business suit and looked like she had just gotten off work. They both ordered meatball subs. I ordered a foot-long veggie delight and an orange juice.

"Steak and cheese foot-long with double meat," said Steve.

He wore jeans and cowboy boots, with an oversize belt buckle that read "Texas." Steve was probably in his mid-fifties and maybe five feet nine—just a bit taller than his wife and daughter. With the boots, though, he was close to my height, six feet two inches. He should have been wearing a cowboy hat, but instead I got to see his graying, closely cropped hair with long sideburns.

"How was the run tonight?" asked Martha as we sat down and started eating.

"Windy," I said. "I was struggling to keep up with your daughter. She's fast."

"Jorge is the fast one," said Alice. "He won the Lake-front 50K a couple of years ago."

"You won your age group?" asked Martha. I get this all the time. I look too old to win races anymore.

"I won overall," I said. "I was forty-six at the time. Second place was twenty-four. I won one for the old guys."

"Impressive," said Martha.

"Well, I was almost twenty pounds lighter back then and much faster," I said.

"Mom, Dad," said Alice. "I was telling Jorge about the Quiznos and all the debt we have now."

I saw Martha's and Steve's faces both sink, and their bodies slump. Steve looked away. I wasn't sure if it was because of embarrassment or shame—probably both. I'd felt it too.

"Hey, I had some big debt problems myself several years ago," I quickly interjected, trying to alleviate their discomfort. "I owned four thousand apartment units across the country and lost everything, ending up twenty-six million dollars in debt." I saw their faces brighten. "I know how it feels."

"I didn't know that you were in that much debt," Alice said, looking at me.

"Somehow, when I share how bad my debt problems were, other people feel better," I said. "They think, 'Well, he owed twenty-six million, I only owe fifty thousand, a million, ten million.' Whatever the number they owe is, it's usually less, so they feel better."

"We owe about two hundred and fifty thousand," said Steve. "So you're right. It does feel better that you owed twenty-six million. That sounds unreal."

"That's a lot," said Martha, smiling widely.

"Welcome to the club," Steve said, standing up and reaching out his hand.

"The Debtors Club," I said, wiping my hands on a napkin and then standing up and shaking Steve's hand. "We've all got to stick together."

I saw Alice break out into a big grin. "So Jorge was telling me that we should stop paying everything. I know it sounds out there, but he said that we can gain leverage if we stop paying and exploit deficiencies. Tell them," she said, looking at me.

I explained how inaccuracies and loopholes could be leveraged to settle debts at big discounts. I noticed Steve nodding.

"You sound just like my DUI attorney," Steve said.

"How so?" I asked before taking a swig of my orange juice.

"I was drunk that night. I admit it. I feel terrible for hurting those two students," Steve said. "I am thankful to God that they recovered."

"Thanks to God," said Martha, as she reached over and clasped Steve's hand.

"But I can't go to prison," Steve said, his face scrunched

with anxiety at the thought. "I am facing one to three years."

"First-time DUI?" I asked.

"Yes," said Steve.

"That sounds like a lot of time for a first offense," I said.

"First time is usually up to a year in prison," said Steve. "But I had fallen behind on my insurance payments, so my coverage had been cancelled when I had the accident. No insurance bumps up the prison time."

"You are not going to prison, Daddy," said Alice, suddenly sounding like a preteen yet trying to reassure her father. She looked distraught.

"I go to the meetings solid now," Steve said. "I'm one hundred and twenty-one days sober. That night was my last drunk." In AA vernacular, "last drunk" is your last big drink-fest—the one that made you realize that you should finally get sober.

"My attorney says that the prosecutor must prove their case beyond a reasonable doubt," Steve said. "He says that the police could have lost or mishandled my DUI evidence, maybe the Breathalyzer was not maintained correctly, maybe they did not follow proper procedure during the arrest, or maybe they violated my rights somehow."

"He sounds like a good attorney," I said.

"We're hopeful," said Martha.

"If we can identify deficiencies, we may be able to get them to agree to a plea deal that's favorable to me, like no prison," said Steve. "Or have the case dismissed completely. It sounds like what you're saying too."

"I never thought about it before," I said. "But that's the same basic process I preach."

"It reminds me of when big-time drug dealers hire expensive lawyers," Alice said. "And then get out of jail on technicalities."

"Same thing," I said, although cleansing unaffordable debt seemed a more noble purpose than getting out of a DUI or drug charge. However, sitting here at Subway with Steve and his family, I didn't want him to go to prison. Surely, a license suspension, a job, some kind of therapy, or just being part of a society in which everyone feels included would be a better and more effective solution.

If we as a society have so many men going to prison, is that the failure of the prisoners, or is that the failure of our society? If we as a society have more than half our population saddled with unaffordable debts, is that the failure of those debtors, or is that the failure of our society? Are the prisoners and debtors bad people, or are they by-products of a broken culture? We are all losing. Something has to change.

"I hope your attorney keeps you out of prison, Steve," I said. "I really do."

"We do, too," said Martha quietly.

"Tell me about the debts," I said.

"The landlord from our Quiznos store went to court to get a judgment," said Steve. "They're trying to levy our bank account. Luckily, there's nothing in it."

"That's helpful," I said.

"I have to go to court next week for some kind of examination," Steve said.

"A debtor's exam," I said. "They call them citations in Illinois." Creditors use debtor's exams and citations to discover what sources of income or property a debtor can use to pay off a judgment. Debtors are summoned to court to answers questions and furnish documents such as tax returns, bank statements, and pay stubs.

"That's it," said Steve. "A citation."

"It's a scary sounding thing, but don't be uncomfortable," I said. "Here's my advice: when it comes to a citation, the strategy is to first, tell the truth. Second, do not elaborate, just answer 'yes' or 'no.' When you must say more, just give basic answers."

"Like Twitter responses?" Alice offered.

"Exactly," I said. "Short with no extra detail. Third, stay present and in the moment the whole way through. Don't get distracted or thrown off. The other attorney may try to act like your friend, or a bully. Either way, they want to get you talking. Do not get chatty. Stay focused and disciplined. Creditors' attorneys are trying to find out any detail leading to income or substantial assets they can turn into cash."

"Sounds like an interrogation," said Steve. "Do I need an attorney?"

"That depends," I said. "If you have nothing to lose, no attorney needed. If you have assets with equity or income you want to protect, then maybe you can justify the expense of an attorney."

"We have the house, but we're underwater on it," Steve said. "The Accord is in my wife's name. Can they get that?"

"Did she cosign on the lease?" I asked.

"No," said Steve.

"The car's safe then," I said. "Do you have any investments, retirement plans, artwork, a boat, or anything of significant value like that?"

"I cashed in all that and sold everything trying to keep the Quiznos going. I lost my car after I wrecked it. I only have two real valuables left in this world," said Steve. "Martha and Alice."

I felt a familial warmth surround that table at Subway. I had no idea when I set out for a run that night that my path would lead me there. I glanced at Alice. She was glowing. I was happy I ended up here.

I texted my wife: "Out to dinner with friends. Back late. I love you."

"The longer you go without the judgment holder collecting anything, the less likely they will be able to collect and the more likely you can settle for a big discount," I said. "Or not pay at all."

"What about my income?" asked Steve. "I've been helping out my brother-in-law at his auto mechanic's shop to help work off some of what I owe him. Eventually, though, I will need to get a real job. What can the judgment holder do then?"

"If the judgment creditor ever gets persistent, you'll want to think about alternative sources of income," I said.

"Alternative sources?" asked Steve.

"Income that is not from wages," I said. "Wages that are paid with payroll checks and W2's are easier for a judgment holder to attach. To make it difficult, consider 1099 income, become self-employed. Maybe start an LLC and have everything paid to the LLC?" A limited liability company can be created for a thousand dollars or so through an attorney or one of the many online services.

"I already have a LLC from the Quiznos," said Steve. "Can I use that?"

"If there are debts owed by that entity, you are probably better to let it die," I said. "Any debts owed by the LLC without personal guarantees will perish with it." That's why personal guarantees are commonly requested from business owners. If the business goes belly-up, then the creditors can attempt to recover the debts from the guarantors.

"I'll start a fresh LLC," said Steve.

"Yes," I said.

"And the judgment creditor can't get to the income?" asked Steve.

"It's much more difficult to intercept," I said. "The money goes to the LLC, but you control when and even *if* you get distributions. The creditor can't force the LLC to pay money to you. If you are under attack by a creditor for some period, then the LLC just accumulates cash and pays expenses, but doesn't pay you. Best of all, no one pays the judgment holder."

"What happens in the end?" asked Steve.

"The judgment holder eventually gets tired and becomes receptive to settling at a big discount," I said. "Or they just move on and focus resources on other debtors who are not giving them so much trouble.

"What about bank accounts?"

"Don't keep big money in any bank account in your name," I said. "Carry some cash, and store any extra money with PayPal."

"PayPal?" asked Steve. "Can't they get that?"

"Yes, they can," I said. "But they rarely ask for it as part of their citation or exam. They ask for bank accounts and whatever other questions they've been asking for years. Asking if you have PayPal or an alternative currency such as Bitcoin is not typically in their repertoire, at least not yet."

"Sounds like creditors' attorneys need to update their questions," said Martha.

"Yes, they're slow adapters," I said. "If they did ask, you could just spend the money online that day. Buy Amazon gift cards if needed. You can use those for just about anything."

"This sounds like a game of cat and mouse," asked Alice.

"That's right," I said. "Just wait for the cat to get tired of chasing you and then offer a little kibble to get him to go away. What other debts you got?" I said. "Line 'em up."

"That's what I used to say before I got drunk at the bar," said Steve, frowning.

"Oh, I am so sorry," I said. "I didn't mean anything."

"No, it's fine," said Steve. "We owe the Quiznos supply affiliate over sixty thousand dollars...with a personal guarantee."

"Fuck Quiznos," said Martha, raising her bottle of iced tea. We all raised our drinks together in a toast.

"Fuck Quiznos!" we said in unison.

The cashier gave us a confused look, which we all caught.

"Yay Subway," volunteered Alice. We all raised our beverages again.

"Yay Subway!" we all said in unison.

The cashier smiled, but still appeared puzzled.

"Treat that Quiznos debt like any unsecured debt," I said. "Ignore them, save the correspondence, log the calls. Wait to see if they try to sue you. If they do, ask for all their documents and records, and make them prove every penny you allegedly owe. Exploit any shortcomings."

"They were overcharging us," said Steve.

"Put together all the records you have now; write down a summary while everything's relatively fresh in your head,"

I said. "You'll have everything ready if they try to sue. Plus, if they were overcharging, maybe you can countersue."

I found out later that Quiznos paid $95 million in 2010 to 6,900 franchisees to settle allegations of overcharging by their affiliated supplier. Close to a dozen new lawsuits were filed in the last two years alleging that (per one suit) "the hidden mark-ups, which are the keystone of Quiznos' scheme, have generated massive profits for Quiznos while simultaneously driving its franchisees to financial ruin." Most of the suits contain identical or similar language.

"What else do you have?" I asked.

"SBA loan," Steve said, "about one hundred thousand dollars with a personal guarantee." The SBA obtains guarantees on many loans so that they can look to recover from personal assets if the business is unable to repay the loan. The default rate for Quiznos franchisees on SBA loans is close to 30 percent, among the worst rates for franchise borrowers. At the other end of the spectrum, Subway franchisees default less than 8 percent of the time, which is among the best rates for franchisees.

"I hate those personal guarantees," I said. "At the time you sign, you think there is no way you are going to fail. But when something happens, you have these massive debts hanging over you."

"When we started, I never contemplated that our shop could fail," said Steve.

"SBA loans are like student loans," I said. "You could

get a private collection agency or the government pursuing you. Either way, the goal is the same: find technicalities to get you out of the debt. Just like big-time drug dealers do to get out of jail." I looked at Alice and we both grinned.

"Treat the private collectors just like the Quiznos affiliate," I said. "However, if the government tries to collect through the Treasury Department, they may add a collection fee of up to thirty percent." This is similar to the collection fees charged on student loans.

"Thirty percent," said Martha. "Thirty percent of the amount you owe?"

"Yes," I said. "They take an unaffordable debt and make it even more unaffordable."

"No wonder the economy is in shambles," said Martha. "Why would anyone take a risk and take on debt to start a business in such a bad economy when the risk is so high? It's safer to stay at a poor-paying job."

"The key is to not take on debt when you start a business," I said. "Your chances of success are much higher." I thought back to when my partner, Darin, and I each kicked in fifty dollars to start Sunset Mortgage twenty-two years ago. We never put in another dime, and the business is still going strong today.

"Don't you usually need money to start a business?" asked Martha.

"There are many businesses you can start with little money and then reinvest the earnings to grow," I said.

"Steve, you work on cars. Have you heard of those GPS disabler devices that dealers put on financed cars?"

"Yeah, I heard of those," he said. "They let Big Brother follow you around all day."

"Could you remove one?" I asked.

"Sure," Steve said. "That's probably easy, but wouldn't that be illegal?"

"Dealers imply that it's illegal," I said. "It's not. The owner of the car can take them out, or hire someone to. Do you have the tools to do it?" I asked.

"That should take just basic tools," said Steve. "I should have what I need or could buy for less than fifty dollars."

"Put an ad on Craigslist tonight saying you will remove those devices for one hundred dollars," I said. "I bet you'll get all kinds of people willing to pay you one hundred dollars. If you do good quality work, are reliable, and charge fairly, you will have started what should be a successful business. The demand for this service is likely to boom."

"No debt needed," said Steve wide-eyed as if a curtain had been opened to a new frontier.

"Exactly," I said. "You can start tonight when you go home and post online. Don't start an LLC yet though. Just take on a few jobs to earn enough to pay for the cost of creating an LLC. And if you like, you can post the service for free on debtcleanse.com to get more clients."

"What about a business plan and stuff like that?" asked Martha.

"The plan is for Steve to remove these devices, charge a fair price, and get good word of mouth," I said. "The next day, he does the same. You don't need a business plan or financials for that. Those are only needed if he was going after a loan."

"Debt killed my business like it is now killing Quiznos," Steve said. "So no debt is the key to a successful business?"

"Plenty of successful businesses have debt," I said. "However, if you start a business with debt, your chances of failing increase significantly. Besides, so many people who want to start a business waste tons of time and money completing business plans and projections. They need to just start the business with what they have, earn some money, and then reinvest that money into the business to grow."

"Our financial projections for our Quiznos store showed that we would make a lot of money relatively quickly," said Steve. "I guess they didn't really help."

"You'll make more removing GPS devices than you did running that Quiznos," I said. "Even better, when the SBA and your other creditors try to collect, if you utilize an LLC, they will have difficulty attacking what you make."

"Sounds good," said Steve.

"Still, the SBA may try to keep your tax refund, or even take your Social Security in the future," I said. "They can even garnish wages and levy your accounts without getting a judgment."

"That sounds terrible," said Martha

"It is. There's good news, though," I said. "They need to send you a notice before they take any of those actions. In the notice, you are invited to request an administrative hearing and request documents."

"Invited," Steve said, chuckling. "Let me guess, the Treasury doesn't have all the documents and records either, so you exploit deficiencies to get a discounted settlement."

"Or pay nothing," said Martha.

"You're learning," I said, smiling. "However, you often need to get into court and gain leverage in order to maximize the discount."

"Can you excuse me? I need to get another sandwich," Alice said. "The run really built up my appetite. Anyone else want anything?"

"I'll get something else, too," I said. We both got up, walked to the counter, and ordered.

"Thanks for talking with my parents," said Alice. "I haven't seen them this happy in a long time. Usually, they don't want to talk about this stuff."

"I'm glad to help," I said. "They're both really nice people." I glanced back at Alice's parents. They appeared to be in a heated discussion. Steve looked upset.

"Thanks," said Alice. We returned to the table and started eating. I unwrapped my second foot-long veggie delight of the night. I was starving.

"How'd you get like this?" asked Steve, looking at me.

His face appeared to have hardened.

"Like what?" I asked. I wasn't sure, but it sounded like he was accusing me of something.

"You seem like a real smart guy," he said. "But your passion seems to be telling people how to not pay their debts."

"To not pay their *unaffordable* debts," I corrected him.

"What's in it for you?" he asked.

"I'm not looking for anything from you," I said, feeling defensive but unsure what I did.

"Dad," said Alice, exasperated. "Leave him be. He's only trying to help."

"You're not alone in your struggles," I said. "The majority of Americans have unaffordable debts. Everyone deserves to know how to come out from under it."

"What kind of life is it to tell others to not pay their debts?" said Steve.

"It's what I'm good at," I said. "I want to help families like yours."

"Is that something to be proud of, being a deadbeat and telling everyone else to be deadbeats, too?" said Steve.

What happened to the Debtors Club? I thought.

"Steve, leave him alone," said Martha, as she put her hand firmly on Steve's shoulder to try to settle him down.

"I'm sorry," I heard Alice say. She sounded dismayed.

My eyes met Steve's. His were hazel, like Alice's. I could tell he'd had some tough times, and there was some contamination in his head. As our gaze stuck, I guessed he probably thought the same about me—at least the tough times part. Men tend to keep bad thoughts, sadness, and pain buried deep inside.

You'll be able to get it out, I tried to tell him with my eyes. *Just let some time pass.*

"You guys having a staring contest?" asked Alice, trying to lighten the mood.

"No," said Steve, sounding calmer. "We're just getting to know each other."

"We're okay," I said.

"Tell me what happened to you," Steve said, still sullen, but warmer.

I told the Woodland Meadows story. I confided everything, trying to get a bit more of the contamination out of my head. My tablemates appeared to be listening intently. I wasn't sure how they were interpreting my history.

"My dream is for millions of families to collectively rid themselves of unaffordable debt. It's my life's passion—the reason I believe I'm here—to show them how they can do it. I don't believe anyone deserves to go through what I went through and what you're going through, especially not over the course of their entire lives."

I had told this story before, but I had never told the *entire* story to anyone but Verria. I felt good as I finished releasing my own history, my fears, and my frustration, which I had carried in me for a long time.

We sat in awkward silence for several minutes. I wasn't

sure what Steve was thinking. I realized that I was in Subway after 10:00 p.m. and still dressed in my running gear. My relaxing workout hadn't gone as planned.

"How can we help?" Steve finally asked. His face was relaxed.

I wasn't sure how to answer. I'm usually the one offering to help. Rarely did it ever occur to me to ask for help, or even admit when I needed it. I needed Steve to spread the word to others.

"Follow the Debt Cleanse steps I gave you," I said. "And then share your story. Tell it to anyone who will listen—anyone you think might need it to come out from their unaffordable debt. It's my goal to cleanse all the unaffordable debt millions of Americans already have and to teach them never to use credit again. But I can't do it alone. I need your help."

As I said it, I knew it was true. We can do it if we all come together—a sea of American debtors forming a giant, powerful wave that wipes out the debt in our lives to create a better, brighter future. The future we've envisioned. The future we deserve. But I can't do it alone. I need your help.

ABOUT THE AUTHOR

JORGE P. NEWBERY is a successful entrepreneur, distressed debt and real estate investor, endurance athlete, and author. He turned around some of the country's must troubled housing complexes by amassing a portfolio of four thousand apartments across the United States from 1992 to 2005. Today, Newbery helps others crushed by unaffordable debts rebuild their lives. He is the founder and CEO of American Homeowner Preservation, a socially responsible debt buyer that purchases nonperforming mortgages from banks at big discounts and then shares the discounts with families. He also founded DebtCleanse.com, which helps debtors and creditors settle unaffordable debts at discounts.

Made in the USA
Charleston, SC
25 October 2016